Build Your Own
home office
furniture

POPULAR WOODWORKING BOOKS

CINCINNATI, OHIO

www.popularwoodworking.com

! Read This Important Safety Notice

To prevent accidents, keep safety in mind while you work. Use the safety guards installed on power equipment; they are for your protection. When working on power equipment, keep fingers away from saw blades, wear safety goggles to prevent injuries from flying wood chips and saw-dust, wear headphones to protect your hearing, and consider installing a dust vacuum to reduce the amount of airborne sawdust in your woodshop. Don't wear loose clothing, such as neckties or shirts with loose sleeves, or jewelry, such as rings, necklaces or bracelets, when working on power equipment. Tie back long hair to prevent it from getting caught in your equipment. People who are sensitive to certain chemicals should check the chemical content of any product before using it. The author and editors who compiled this book have tried to make the contents as accurate and correct as possible. Plans, illustrations, photographs and text have been carefully checked. All instructions, plans and projects should be carefully read, studied and understood before beginning construction. Due to the variability of local conditions, construction materials, skill levels, etc., neither the author nor Popular Woodworking Books assumes any responsibility for any accidents, injuries, damages or other losses incurred resulting from the material presented in this book.

METRIC CONVERSION CHART

TO CONVERT	TO	MULTIPLY BY
Inches	Centimeters	2.54
Centimeters	Inches	0.4
Feet	Centimeters	30.5
Centimeters	Feet	0.03
Yards	Meters	0.9
Meters	Yards	1.1
Sq. Inches	Sq. Centimeters	6.45
Sq. Centimeters	Sq. Inches	0.16
Sq. Feet	Sq. Meters	0.09
Sq. Meters	Sq. Feet	10.8
Sq. Yards	Sq. Meters	0.8
Sq. Meters	Sq. Yards	1.2
Pounds	Kilograms	0.45
Kilograms	Pounds	2.2
Ounces	Grams	28.4
Grams	Ounces	0.04

Library of Congress Cataloging-in-Publication Data

Proulx, Danny
    Build your own home office furniture / Danny Proulx.
       p. cm.
    Includes index.
    ISBN 1-55870-561-9
     1. Furniture making. 2. Office furniture. I. Title.

TT197 .P7598 2001
684.1--dc21

2001021616

TT197
.P7598
2001

Edited by Jennifer Churchill
Content edited by Michael Berger
Cover designed by Brian Roeth
Interior designed by Andrea Short
Interior layout produced by Ben Rucker
Production coordinated by Mark Griffin

CREDITS:

Step-by-Step Photography by:
Danny Proulx

Step-by-Step Photography,
chapters 13 and 14, by:
Jim Stack

Cover and Chapter Lead
Photography by:
Michael Bowie
Lux Photography
2450 Lancaster Rd., Suite 25
Ottawa, Ontario, Canada
K1B 5N3
613-247-7199

Chapter Lead Photography,
chapters 13 and 14, by:
Al Parrish

Computer Illustrations by:
Len Churchill
Lenmark Communications Ltd.
590 Alden Rd., Suite 206
Markham, Ontario, Canada
L3R 8N2
905-475-5222

Workshop Site:
Rideau Cabinets
P.O. Box 331
Russell, Ontario, Canada
K4R 1E1
613-445-3722

Acquisitions Editor:
Jim Stack

[danny proulx]

about the Author

Danny Proulx has been involved in the woodworking field for more than 30 years. He has operated a custom kitchen cabinet shop since 1989.

He is a contributing editor to *CabinetMaker* magazine and has published articles in other magazines such as *Canadian Home Workshop*, *Canadian Woodworking*, *Popular Woodworking*, *Woodshop News* and *Homes & Cottages*.

His books include *Build Your Own Kitchen Cabinets*, *The Kitchen Cabinetmaker's Building and Business Manual*, *How to Build Classic Garden Furniture*, *Smart Shelving and Storage Solutions*, *Building Modern Cabinetry* and *Building More Classic Garden Furniture*.

Visit Danny's Web site at www.cabinetmaking.com. He can be reached by e-mail at danny@cabinetmaking.com.

[dedication]

This book is another team effort. I couldn't meet deadlines, build *and* write without the dedicated help of my wife, Gale, and my shop assistant, Jack Chaters. The master of photographic art, Michael Bowie of Lux Photography in Ottawa, is the wizard behind the images. Len Churchill, of Lenmark Communications in Markham, has again provided the exploded views. Len is a genius with illustrations.

The staff at Popular Woodworking Books is my support team; I'm very lucky to have such a talented and dedicated group of professionals that includes Michael Berger, Jennifer Churchill, Emily Gross and a dozen other stars.

I want to particularly thank PW's editorial team leader Jim Stack. He not only supported me along the way — doing the extraordinary — he designed and built the two great desks in chapters thirteen and fourteen. He is a talented individual. Thanks Jim!

[acknowledgements]

There have been many suppliers who have contributed products, material and technical support during the project-building phase. I appreciate how helpful they've been and recommend these companies without hesitation.

Julius Blum Inc.
800-438-6788
www.blum.com

Delta International Machinery Corp.
800-438-2486
www.deltawoodworking.com

LRH Enterprises Inc.
800-423-2544
www.lrhent.com

Rout-R-Slide
Jessem Tool Co.
800-436-6799
www.jessem.com

Please refer to the "Sources" page for a complete list of companies.

[table of contents]

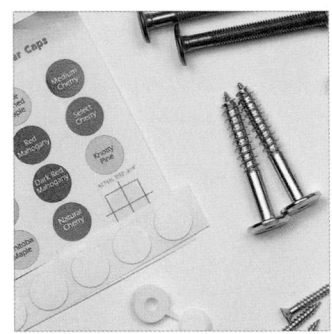

Introduction

Many of the projects in this book will be built using modern sheet goods — material such as medium-density fiberboard (MDF), veneer and coated particleboard (PB), and veneer-covered plywoods. These materials are the perfect choice for a number of reasons. First, they are uniform in size and thickness, stable, ready to use, and have companion hardware that is used to join these products. But most importantly, these sheet goods sustain our forests and don't deplete our natural timber resources like solid wood. MDF, PB, and the plycore veneers use, in many cases, scrub trees that grow quickly. These so-called "waste" trees were plowed under or burnt in the past but have now become a useful and cost-effective resource.

There are purists who turn their noses up at the thought of building with composite materials. But a good part of an old-growth tree is needed to build a solid wood desk. You can build the desk with "waste" trees that are used to make particleboard and achieve almost identical results. It's just as strong and looks just as nice! And, you've helped manage our forests.

The Learning Process

I enjoy writing books about woodworking. To work at something I love and being able to make a living is a real pleasure. However, putting these books together so you can simply follow the building plans isn't my real purpose. My goal is to try to teach something new in each book. Simply following building plans will result in a beautiful project. But if you haven't learned anything in the process all you have is a piece of furniture. Learning new skills and techniques is the ultimate goal — it's a priceless accomplishment and much more valuable than any piece of furniture.

As I often tell my students, focus on the "why" of each step, not on the final result. And ask questions! The only so-called "dumb" question is the one that wasn't asked! I'm always available via e-mail at danny@cabinetmaking.com.

The Projects

The first chapter details some of the modern fastening devices and materials that have been developed for composite material joinery. This book is all about practical furniture — reasonably priced, well-built and, above all else, functional. This modern hardware lets us accomplish these goals and the results are impressive.

The heart of many home office furniture pieces is a flat work surface. In chapter two, you'll learn how particleboard, high-pressure laminates and a little bit of solid wood can be formed to make the perfect desktop. Laminates are available in sheet sizes up to 5' x 12'. So, the worktable top can be made to suit any requirement. The colors are numerous and you can form any shape you need.

In chapter three, you'll learn how to build modules to support the desktop. These modules can be storage drawers, file drawers, compartments with doors or a combination of the three. You can build any configuration by combining the wood-edged top and two or three custom modules.

The rest of the projects can make any home office both functional and attractive. From lateral file cabinets to bookcases to complete workstations, there's a project for every need and space requirement. There's even a self-contained armoire that opens up into a complete office!

We have CDs, VHS tapes, back-up tapes, books and other items that need media storage devices. Where do we keep all that data? Take a look at the media storage center in chapter eleven. It might be the answer to your media storage needs.

Chapter twelve details the possibilities for converting that unused closet into a dynamic home office. It's another work center that can be hidden quickly when your workday is done.

The last two projects were designed and built by editor Jim Stack of Popular Woodworking Books. Jim is just one of the many great editors and extremely talented woodworkers that I've encountered on the PW staff.

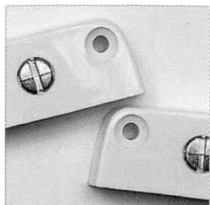

[c h a p t e r   o n e]

modern Materials & Hardware

The last few years have been exciting for those in the building materials and hardware business. Modern plywood, improved particleboard (PB), melamine-coated particleboard (MPB) and medium-density fiberboard (MDF) have tremendously affected the way we build cabinets for our homes and offices.

We now realize our forest products must be managed carefully. Wood once burned or discarded is now seen as a valuable resource. Improved management of that wood has been a blessing to all of us who care about our forests.

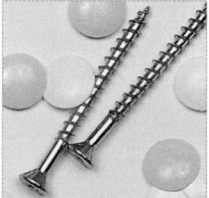

Modern Materials

Particleboard (PB) and medium-density fiberboard (MDF) have become popular as a cabinet-making material in the commercial casework industry and are now being accepted by the hobbyist woodworker. Some of you may have tried these composite boards when they were first introduced and may have been disappointed. But today's products are far superior to the early offerings.

Low-cost sheet material, though available, isn't a good value for your money and should be avoided. Ask for cabinet-grade products and pay a little more to get high-quality material. Most often, it's only a few dollars more per sheet, but it's well worth the money. For example, melamine particleboard (MPB) is graded 100, 120 or 140 for cabinet construction. You can make a lot of furniture from one sheet of MPB, so a few extra dollars isn't a major issue.

Joinery Techniques

The butt joint, made using modern hardware, is the most common joinery method. But most adhesives are not suited for properly joining many of the modern coated materials. For example, melamine, which is paper soaked in resins and fused to PB, cannot be glued with standard wood adhesives. Therefore, we depend on high-quality fasteners to build our cabinets.

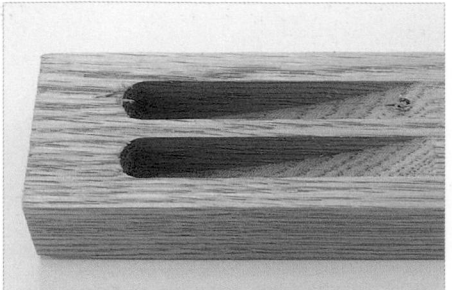

POCKET HOLES
Newer style joinery, such as the "pocket hole" joint, has gained wide acceptance. Low-cost jigs are available to help you quickly and accurately master this joint.

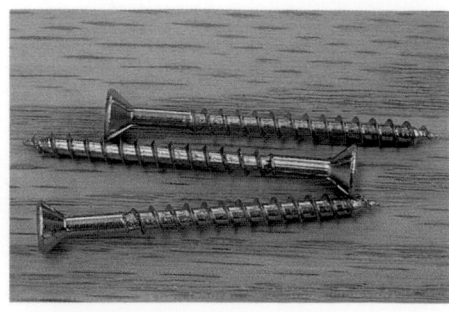

CHIPBOARD SCREWS
The PB (or chipboard) screw is the preferred fastener when joining PB material. PB screws are available from most hardware suppliers. They have a thin shaft with a coarse thread and are specially designed to hold PB securely.

SCREW CAPS
Other decorative screws for PB have screw-on caps that are available in many finishes. These caps can be matched to complement the coated PB surface — and, when properly located on the project, look great.

HOLE COVERINGS
When working with wood-veneer-covered PB, we have dozens of wood-screw hole coverings available. The plug and button are the two common types, but there are many other styles available.

PLASTIC SCREW COVERS
Plastic screw cover caps are a popular way to conceal screw heads. Some are held on by the screw; some are push-on styles, while others are glued in place. Whichever style you choose, you'll be able to match almost any material finish imaginable.

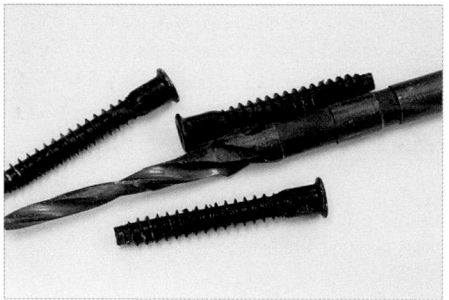

SPECIALIZED SCREWS
There is a special PB screw available that, until recently, has only been used by professional cabinetmakers. It's a great fastener, but there are a couple of issues you should be aware of. First, the screw is tapered and requires a special, and somewhat expensive, drill bit. Secondly, because of its large diameter and coarse thread, you must drill accurate pilot holes and drive the screw straight for a positive hold. Poor drilling or improper driving will push the screw through the finished surface or weaken the joint.

KNOCKDOWN HARDWARE

Furniture that can be taken apart is a necessary requirement for some people. That need has led to the development of a whole range of joinery bolts that allow for quick disassembly without damage. Cabinet and furniture makers have developed many applications for this type of fastener. It's often seen on children's beds and storage shelving systems. The Europeans have expanded the use of these bolts and developed an extensive line of knock-down furniture.

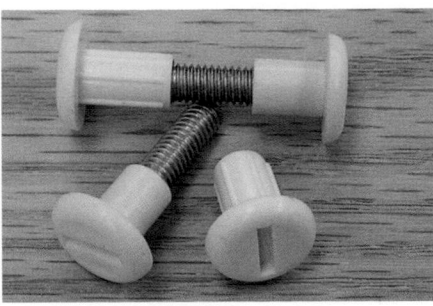

PLASTIC DECORATIVE BOLTS

A plastic-covered version of the decorative bolt is often found in frameless kitchen cabinets. Frameless kitchen cabinet builders use a form of these bolts to secure the front edges of cabinets. The plastic-covered styles are also used in commercial cabinet applications.

DECORATIVE END CAPS

Another version of decorative bolt joinery uses a finished end cap. The bolt is often hidden and only the cap is visible. The head is about ½" in diameter and is drawn tight to the material surface. These cap nuts provide a sound mechanical connection. They are also used on high-stress joints such as bed frames.

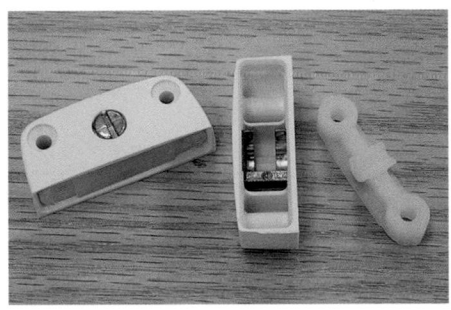

SPECIALIZED QUICK-CONNECT HARDWARE

Quick-connect hidden hardware is common in some furniture designs. There are many types of quick-connect-and-release right-angle butt joinery hardware items available. Furniture is shipped flat-packed and sold to the consumer with pre-installed quick-connect hardware.

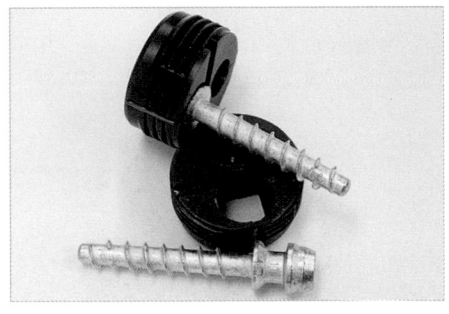

LOCKING CAMS

Some quick-connect hardware requires a hole. Once the locking cam is secured in the hole and the pin is installed in the piece to be joined, a cam is turned to lock the pieces together.

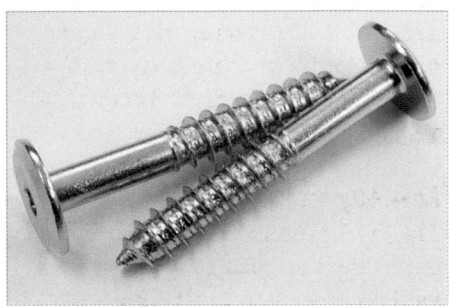

OTHER HARDWARE

I'll use some of these hardware items, such as this decorative PB cap screw, to build a few of the projects in this book. It may not be purist wood-working, but these fasteners do have a place in modern cabinetry. They are fun to use and extremely strong when correctly installed.

Hinges

In the last few years, door-mounting hardware from Europe has become a very popular alternative. The so-called "Euro hidden hinge" is now widely used as the standard kitchen cabinet door hardware.

The hidden hinge usually requires a 35mm hole drilled in the door. That task seems a bit challenging to some people but it's a straightforward process.

There is a learning curve when working with the hidden hinge. For instance, these hinges are classified with terms such as *full overlay* and *half overlay*. That simply means how much the door covers the cabinet side member (gable end). The third type of hinge is an inset style that is used to mount the doors flush with the cabinet face.

Parts of a Hinge

The hidden hinge comes in two parts: the hinge, or boss, which is mounted on the door; and the mounting plate, which is attached to the cabinet side or gable end of the cabinet.

The boss is attached to the mounting plate with a screw or a clip pin (clip-on). The clip-on method is becoming popular because you can remove the door from the mounting plate without disturbing any adjustments.

Degrees of Operation

Hidden hinges are also classed in terms of degrees of opening. For standard door applications, the 100° to 110° opening hinge is common. But you can purchase hinges that will allow the door to open from 90° to 170°. The term simply refers to the number of degrees of swing that the door can open from its closed position.

Other Hardware and Materials

And the list continues endlessly. There are so many exciting products on the market, which means the designs are limited only by your imagination.

Biscuit joinery, pocket holes, new and improved glues, hardware to complement any application and the composite materials that are available

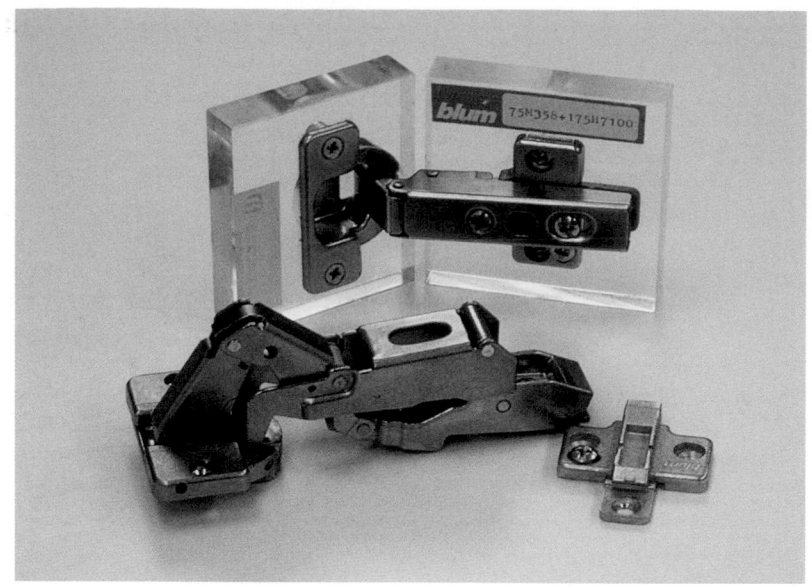

TYPICAL HIDDEN HINGES

ADJUSTABLE SHELVING HARDWARE
The fixed shelf is gone! Nowadays, everyone wants adjustable shelves in their cabinets. It's a feature that makes sense because it increases the flexibility of any cabinet. Adjustable shelving is easy to install. All that is required are accurately drilled columns of holes and good-quality shelf pins. Quite a few of the projects in this book will feature adjustable shelving.

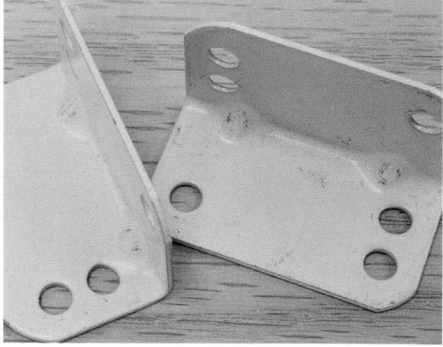

COUNTERTOP ATTACHMENT HARDWARE
Attaching countertops during a kitchen project is often accomplished using metal brackets. It's the best method for securing something, like a kitchen counter top, which will have to be replaced in the future. These brackets come in many shapes and sizes. They provide a quick-connect capability and add strength to any project. They are sometimes used with other joinery hardware to provide extra hold when joint stress is an issue.

open the door to projects that were next to impossible in the past.

These wood products can be easily used in any shop — even the most basic one. Jigs are available to help install the hardware but there are simple tricks that make installation a snap. I'll show you some of these procedures as we go through the projects.

Don't discount these products

because they will allow you to build functional and strong office furniture. They are far removed from a traditional dovetail joint in solid wood, however, these materials do have their place. I've made every type of joint in solid wood over my woodworking life and I can honestly say that I'm having more fun now that I've discovered modern hardware and materials!

DRAWER GLIDES AND HARDWARE

Modern hardware now gives us the opportunity to vary drawer styles and construction methods. Side- and bottom-mount glides with three-quarter and full-extension capabilities, along with positive stops and closing features, have opened a world of design opportunities. Low-cost metal drawer glide sets, which consist of two bottom-mount drawer runners and two cabinet tracks, are simple to install. Installing the new drawer hardware demands special attention to the drawer body width, as most of the hardware requires very precise clearances to operate properly. Otherwise, building high-quality drawers is well within the abilities of any woodworker or hobbyist.

PARTICLEBOARD AND PLYWOOD BOARDS

Particleboard and plywood boards are stable materials that are suitable for many applications. The melamine-coated decorative panels come in a wide range of colors, while wood veneer boards can be stained, glued, joined and used like solid wood.

EDGE TAPE

All of the colored panels and wood veneers have complementary edge tape that is attached with glue.

COLORS AND TEXTURES

There are dozens of decorative panel colors and textures available that will allow you to build prefinished desks and cabinets.

HIGH-PRESSURE LAMINATES

High-pressure laminates are the best materials for kitchen countertops. But there are many other cabinet applications. I'll use some of these materials for the projects in this book and detail the installation procedures.

[modular projects]

These three projects (chapters 2, 3 and 4) offer you the ultimate

in flexibility when planning your own home-office layout. Each of

these units can be sized to fit your needs and space considerations.

[page 15]

[page 22]

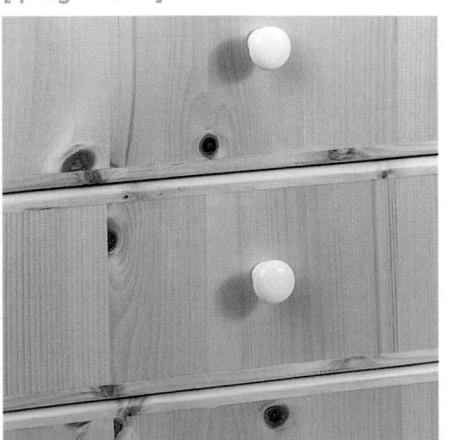

[page 29]

[chapter two]

laminate Tabletop Construction

There is a countertop style that's easily made and well within any woodworker's capabilities. The process involves attaching a wood edge trim to a panel, called the substrate, and covering the top with a high-pressure laminate. These laminates are made with decorative surface papers impregnated with melamine resins that are pressed over kraft paper core sheets. These sheets are then bonded at pressures of 1,000 pounds or more per square inch with temperatures approaching 300°F (149°C). The finished sheets are trimmed and the backs sanded to facilitate bonding. Most manufacturers have over 100 different patterns available.

Building a Laminate Top

There are two thicknesses of high-pressure laminate materials. The thinner version is used to manufacture post-formed countertops that are common in almost every kitchen and bathroom. The thicker general purpose (GP) laminates are used for applications like the top you're about to build here. The GP material is able to stand more abuse because of its thickness.

This great-looking wood-edged countertop style has a number of uses. It can be used as a kitchen or bathroom countertop, a work center/desk or as a utility countertop. I've used it in dozens of unique projects over the years. And, because the laminate is available in 4' × 8' or 5' × 12' sheets, most tops can be made without a seam.

You can use any stable sheet material as the substrate, including PB, plywood and MDF. I would recommend a minimum ¾"-thick substrate for strength and stability. The wood edge can be any hardwood or softwood that matches or complements your cabinets.

Your top can be any dimension that you need, but for this demonstration, we'll use ¾"-thick sheet material (PB, plywood or MDF). We'll also use ¾"-thick by 1½"-high wood edging, as well as the high-pressure laminate for the final surface.

Hardware and Supplies

¾" sheet material: PB, Plywood or MDF

¾" x 1½" wood edging

High-pressure (GP) laminate

Contact cement

[1] Cut the sheet material to the required size. Reduce the desired end size by ¾" where a wood edge will be installed. I am using ¾"-thick PB.

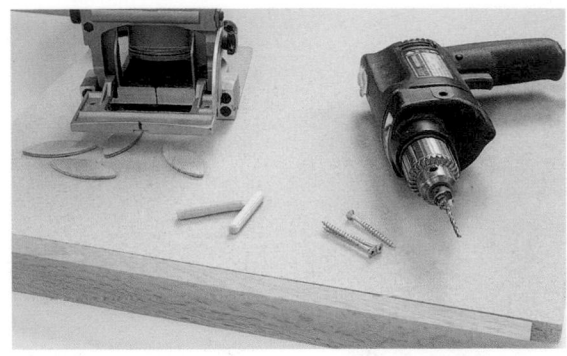

[2] Attach the wood edge with glue and screws covered by wood plugs. You can also use dowels or biscuits — any of these three options will work equally well. Be sure that the top of the wood edge and the surface of the substrate are perfectly flush. If not, sand both to achieve a flat, smooth surface.

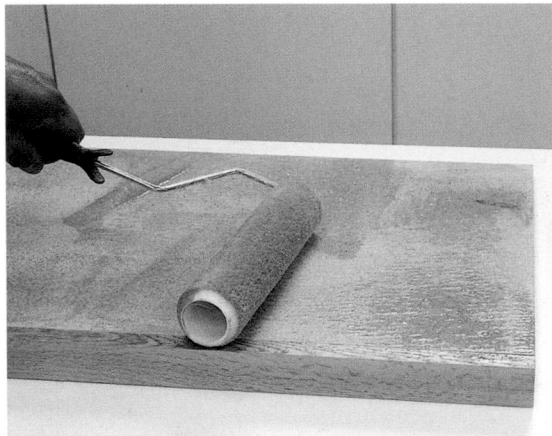

[3] Cut the laminate so it's 1" larger in size than the substrate — the extra width and length will allow for any slight positioning errors. Apply a contact adhesive to both the underside of the laminate and the substrate top. Make certain there's an even coat on both surfaces and all areas are covered. There are many types of contact cement available. I'm using a roller-grade liquid, but there are brush and spray contact cements available at most home stores.

[4] The contact cement is set when it's dry to the touch. However, read the instructions listed on your container for best results. This adhesive will only bond to another surface with the same glue applied. You can place dry sticks on the substrate to keep the materials from touching until the laminate is correctly positioned. Be careful — once the two glued surfaces touch, they are bonded! Remove the center stick and press the laminate in place with your hand. Move your hand from the center to the outside edges to push out any trapped air bubbles.

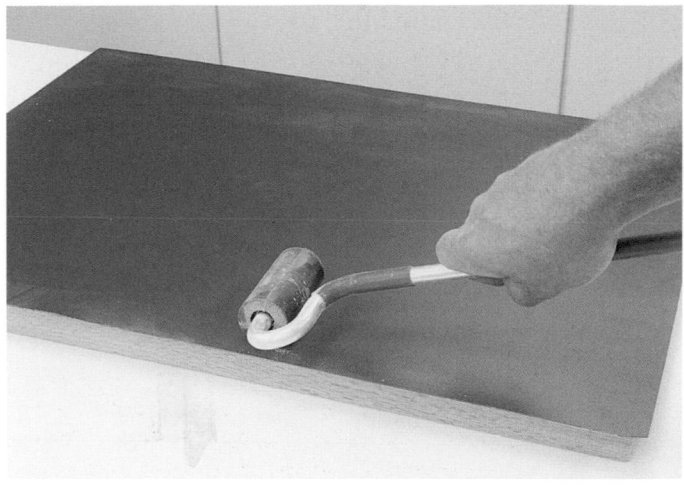

[5] A pressure roller is the best tool to make certain the laminate is completely bonded to the substrate. If you don't have a commercial roller, use a wooden rolling pin or large wooden dowel. Again, roll from the center to the edges and pay particular attention to the laminate edge.

[6] The excess laminate can be cut flush to the wood edge using a flush trim router bit.

[7] A roundover bit in a router is used to make a simple rounded profile on the bottom of the wood edge.

[8] The top or laminated surface of the countertop is cut using the same roundover bit. Set the bit so its straight cutters, which are above the curved portion of the bit, cut slightly lower than the thickness of the laminate material. That cutting pass will expose the wood under the laminate and round the top edge.

Construction Notes

Using GP laminate, which is a thicker material, will provide you with a durable worktop. However, use care when cutting to avoid damaging the laminate. The best router bits are carbide-tipped and work exceptionally well for this application.

The wood edge in my case was oak, but any species can be used. Stick with the major brands of laminate material for the best results. High-quality material and contact cement will give you perfect results every time.

Some adhesives are toxic — particularly petroleum-based products, so work in a well-ventilated area. And make sure to closely follow the application directions from the adhesive manufacturer because heat range and humidity levels are very important when using these products.

A crosscutting sled is one of the handiest and safest table saw accessories you'll ever own. They are simple to build and a real pleasure to use when cutting wide panels.

There are a number of options and safety features that can be added to your crosscutting sled. One woodworker painted the blade guard board red as a reminder of the danger zone near the blade. Some have installed Plexiglas guards above the saw blade path, and a few others have built a small enclosed box on the back of the sled where the blade is exposed when the cut is complete.

I've seen a few sleds that use steel runners much like those on a miter gauge. That's a great feature and it may be worth looking for the runners at your local hardware store.

Finally, if the sled binds, try applying a coat of paste wax to the sled bottom and runners. That should reduce the drag on the table saw top.

Cutting List • Crosscutting Sled

QTY.	PART	THICK	WIDTH	LENGTH
1	Platform	¾	36	30
2	Runners	¾	⅜	30
2	Fences	1½	3½	36
1	Blade guard	1½	3½	10

Metric Cutting List • Crosscutting Sled

QTY.	PART	THICK	WIDTH	LENGTH
1	Platform	19	914	762
2	Runners	19	10	762
2	Fences	38	89	914
1	Blade guard	38	89	254

Hardware and Supplies

Plywood, 2x4 stock

Hardwood or metal runners

Here's the crosscutting sled you'll be building in this demonstration.

[1] Cut the platform to shape, making sure it's accurately sized and square. Then cut the two hardwood runners and test fit them in the table saw miter grooves. A proper fit will allow the runners to run freely with minimal side play. Attach the runners to the platform with 1" screws and glue. Make sure they're properly spaced to match the table saw grooves.

[2] Install the back rail with screws and glue using your saw fence and a framing square to align it at 90° to the fence.

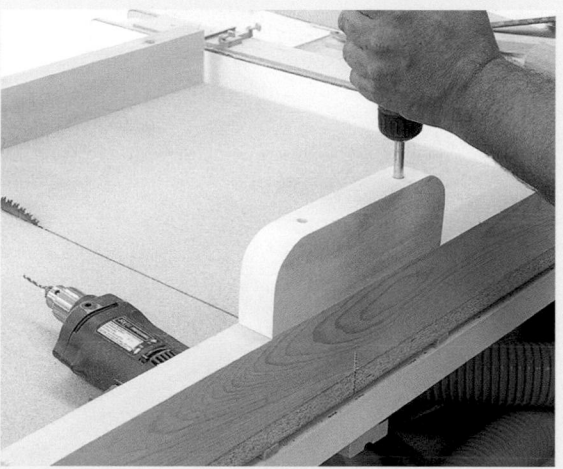

[3] Install the front rail following the same procedures.

[4] Attach the blade guard centered over the blade on the back rail. Round over each end of the guard board with a belt sander to eliminate the sharp corners.

This is a method that I often use to make great-looking raised panel doors on a table saw. But be careful, you will be working near an open unguarded blade. The sample door is 13½" wide by 28" high, but it can be made to any dimension.

Use a heavy-duty blade and make small, slow passes with the door panel. Slower passes will give you a finer cut and eliminate a great deal of final sanding.

The amount you raise the blade for each pass, as well as the travel across the blade, will depend on the wood used. Hardwood will be a lot more difficult than softwood, so make a few trial passes to gauge your speed and cut depth.

Cutting List • Raised Panel Doors

QTY.	PART	THICK	WIDTH	LENGTH
2	Stiles	¾	2¼	28
2	Rails	¾	2¼	10
1	Panel	¾	9⅞	24⅜

Metric Cutting List • Raised Panel Doors

QTY.	PART	THICK	WIDTH	LENGTH
2	Stiles	19	57	711
2	Rails	19	57	254
1	Panel	19	251	620

Hardware and Supplies

Hardwood stiles and rails

Glued-up panels

Glue

Here's a typical raised panel door like the one you'll build in this demonstration.

[1] Prepare the stiles and rails by cutting a groove ¼"-wide by ½"-deep in the middle of one long edge of each piece.

[2] Form a tenon that's ¼"-thick by ½"-long centered on both ends of each rail.

[3] Glue up a number of ¾"-thick boards using biscuits or simple edge gluing. Cut the panel to the size detailed in the cutting list. Next, use the table saw miter gauge to attach a board on the saw at a right angle to the blade. The board can be clamped or attached with screws. The straight edge of the board should cross the center of the blade when it's just below the table surface.

[4] Turn on the saw and raise the blade ½". Push the panel blank across the blade, cutting all four edges starting with the ends on each pass. Raise the blade by ½₂" on each pass. Take it slow and use a push pad. Slow travel across the blade will yield a fine cut.

[5] Continue making passes on all four edges of the door center panel until the edge is slightly smaller than ¼". Sand the panel to remove all saw marks. Test fit the panel in the stiles and rails until you achieve a snug, but not tight, fit. Assemble the door using glue on the tenons only. Do not glue the panel, as it must float freely to account for expansion and contraction during humidity changes.

file & storage Drawer Module

These modules can be customized with any drawer and door size combination. They are perfect support for the wood edged laminate worktop in chapter two.

As previously discussed, laminates are available in 4' × 8' and 5' × 12' sheets. You can make the perfect custom work center for your home office when you combine the top with two or more of these modules.

There are a few rules to follow when building work centers. Normal desk height is 30" to the top surface and the seat is commonly 12" to 18" less than that. If you want a higher worktable, add 6" to the module height and use 24" stools.

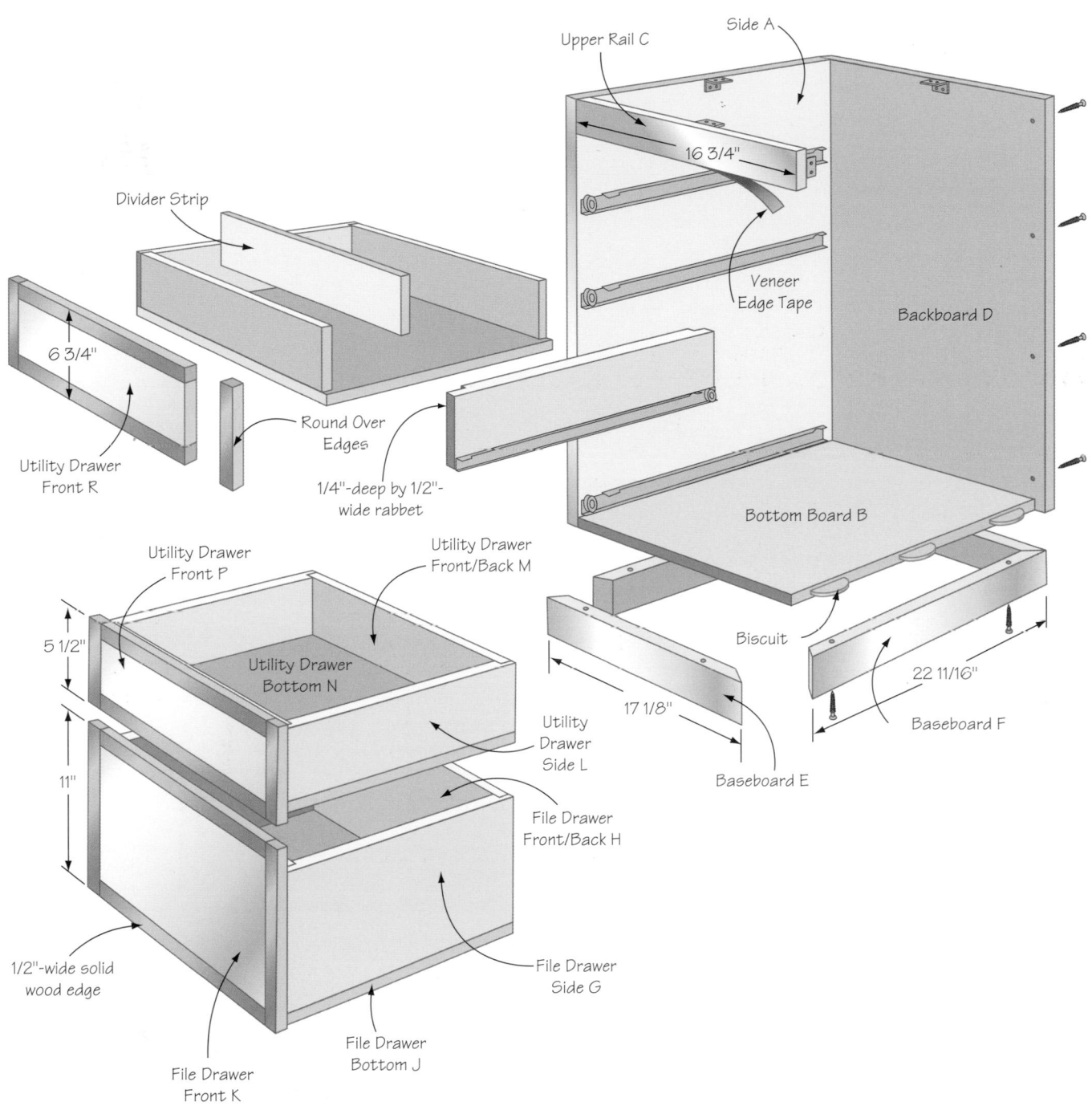

Upper Rail C

Side A

Divider Strip

16 3/4"

Veneer
Edge Tape

Backboard D

6 3/4"

Round Over
Edges

Utility Drawer
Front R

1/4"-deep by 1/2"-
wide rabbet

Bottom Board B

Biscuit

Utility Drawer
Front P

Utility Drawer
Front/Back M

Utility Drawer
Bottom N

22 11/16"

Baseboard F

5 1/2"

Utility
Drawer
Side L

17 1/8"

11"

File Drawer
Front/Back H

Baseboard E

1/2"-wide solid
wood edge

File Drawer
Side G

File Drawer
Front K

File Drawer
Bottom J

Cutting List • File & Storage Drawer Module

REF.	QTY.	PART	MATERIAL	THICKNESS	WIDTH	LENGTH	COMMENTS
A	2	Sides	Veneer PB	$1\frac{1}{16}$	23	$27\frac{3}{4}$	
B	1	Bottom board	Veneer PB	$1\frac{1}{16}$	$16\frac{3}{4}$	23	
C	1	Upper rail	Veneer PB	$1\frac{1}{16}$	2	$16\frac{3}{4}$	
D	1	Backboard	Veneer PB	$1\frac{1}{16}$	$18\frac{1}{8}$	$27\frac{3}{4}$	
E	2	Baseboards	Solid wood	$\frac{3}{4}$	$1\frac{1}{2}$	$17\frac{1}{8}$	Angle cut
F	2	Baseboards	Solid wood	$\frac{3}{4}$	$1\frac{1}{2}$	$22\frac{11}{16}$	Angle cut

File Drawer

REF.	QTY.	PART	MATERIAL	THICKNESS	WIDTH	LENGTH	COMMENTS
G	2	Sides	Baltic birch ply	$\frac{1}{2}$	8	22	
H	2	Front and back	Baltic birch ply	$\frac{1}{2}$	8	$15\frac{1}{4}$	
J	1	Drawer bottom	Baltic birch ply	$\frac{1}{2}$	$15\frac{3}{4}$	22	
K	1	Drawer front	Veneer PB	$1\frac{1}{16}$	11	$16\frac{3}{4}$	With $\frac{1}{2}$"-wide solid wood edges

Utility Drawers

REF.	QTY.	PART	MATERIAL	THICKNESS	WIDTH	LENGTH	COMMENTS
L	4	Sides	Baltic birch ply	$\frac{1}{2}$	5	22	
M	4	Front and back	Baltic birch ply	$\frac{1}{2}$	5	$15\frac{1}{4}$	
N	2	Drawer bottom	Baltic birch ply	$\frac{1}{2}$	$15\frac{3}{4}$	22	
P	1	Drawer front middle	Veneer PB	$1\frac{1}{16}$	$5\frac{1}{2}$	$16\frac{3}{4}$	With $\frac{1}{2}$"-wide solid wood edges
R	1	Drawer front top	Veneer PB	$1\frac{1}{16}$	$6\frac{3}{4}$	$16\frac{3}{4}$	With $\frac{1}{2}$"-wide solid wood edges

Hardware and Supplies

Iron-on veneer	Finishing nails	File hanging hardware or $\frac{1}{8}$"-thick flat metal
Wood tape	22" three-quarter extension bottom-mount drawer glides	Glue
Particleboard	22" full-extension drawer glides	Drawer handles
Screws	Metal right-angle brackets	

Metric Cutting List • File & Storage Drawer Module

REF.	QTY.	PART	MATERIAL	THICKNESS	WIDTH	LENGTH	COMMENTS
A	2	Sides	Veneer PB	18	584	705	
B	1	Bottom board	Veneer PB	18	425	584	
C	1	Upper rail	Veneer PB	18	51	425	
D	1	Backboard	Veneer PB	18	461	705	
E	2	Baseboards	Solid wood	19	38	435	Angle cut
F	2	Baseboards	Solid wood	19	38	577	Angle cut

File Drawer

REF.	QTY.	PART	MATERIAL	THICKNESS	WIDTH	LENGTH	COMMENTS
G	2	Sides	Baltic birch ply	13	203	559	
H	2	Front and back	Baltic birch ply	13	203	387	
J	1	Drawer bottom	Baltic birch ply	13	400	559	
K	1	Drawer front	Veneer PB	18	279	425	With 13mm-wide solid wood edges

Utility Drawers

REF.	QTY.	PART	MATERIAL	THICKNESS	WIDTH	LENGTH	COMMENTS
L	4	Sides	Baltic birch ply	13	127	559	
M	4	Front and back	Baltic birch ply	13	127	387	
N	2	Drawer bottom	Baltic birch ply	13	400	559	
P	1	Drawer front middle	Veneer PB	18	140	425	With 13mm-wide solid wood edges
R	1	Drawer front top	Veneer PB	18	171	425	With 13mm-wide solid wood edges

[Before You Begin]

- **This project shows you how to** build regular storage drawers as well as legal file folder drawers. The file drawers are designed to hold hanging file folders, and the normal inside width of the drawer box is 14¾". The drawer should be 8" deep and provide about 11" of clearance so the files can be seen and handled.

- **Many of the projects in this book** will use a frameless-style cabinet. When building a face-frame style, you would normally cover the cabinet box edges with solid wood. In frameless cabinetry, veneer edge tape is used to finish the box edges that are exposed. Frameless cabinetry is simple to build and less expensive than face frame cabinetry. But if constructed properly, it's just as sturdy.

- **Another common element throughout** this book will be the use of Baltic birch plywood for the drawer boxes. Sometimes called "cabinet-grade plywood," this ½"-thick material has layers that are void free. The layers are often alternated with a dark/light arrangement and they can be sanded smooth. All that's required is a coat of polyurethane to protect the drawers.

TIP

Some species of wood edge tape can be easily trimmed with a sharp knife or double-edge trimmer. The pine I'm using is an example of a close-grained wood that is easily trimmed. Other wood types, such as oak, have a wide grain and tend to "run" in the grain direction and be difficult to trim. For those wood types I use a flush-trim bit in a router.

[1] Cut the two sides and the bottom board. Apply a wood edge pre-glued iron-on veneer edge tape to the front edge of each board.

[2] Join the sides to the bottom board. The lower surface of the bottom board is installed flush with the bottom edge of each side. There are a number of joinery options at this point. I'm using biscuits, glue and clamps to attach the three boards. You can use 2" PB screws in pilot holes that are counterbored and filled with wood plugs or dowels and glue.

[3] While the sides are clamped to the bottom board, cut the rail (C) and apply veneer tape to one long edge. This will be the bottom edge of the rail. Use glue and install the rail so its top edge is even with the side board top edges. Reinforce the joint with two right-angle brackets that are secured with ⅝" screws.

[4] Attach the backboard (D) using 2"-long PB screws and glue. Apply veneer tape to both long edges prior to installation. My module will be against the wall, so screws are acceptable. But if the back will be visible, use biscuits or dowels. The screw method can be used, and the heads hidden, by counterbored holes that are filled with wood plugs.

[5] The base is made using 1x2 solid wood. Join the corners with 45° miters and construct the base frame so it's ½" smaller than the cabinet on all edges. This method will allow the weight to be transferred through the sideboards, onto the solid wood base frame, and then to the floor. Secure the frame with two 1½"-long PB screws through each baseboard, in countersunk holes, and into the bottom board. Use glue to further strengthen the joint.

[6] Cut the two drawer sides (G). The ends of both sides require a ¼"-deep by ½"-wide rabbet. Use a router table or a table saw to complete this cut. Join the sides to the front and back boards, in the rabbets, using glue and 1½" finishing nails.

[7] The bottom board (J) is glued and nailed with 1½" finishing nails to form a drawer box.

[8] I am using Blum 22" bottom-mount drawer glides for my cabinet. These slides will allow the drawer box to pull out three-quarters of their length. If you need the drawer to pull out of the cabinet fully, use full-extension drawer glides.

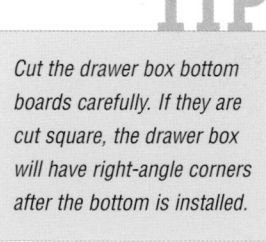

TIP

Cut the drawer box bottom boards carefully. If they are cut square, the drawer box will have right-angle corners after the bottom is installed.

[9] Build the utility drawers following the same procedures as previously described for the file drawer box.

[10] Follow the manufacturer's installation instructions when installing the drawer hardware. You can use a framing square to accurately locate the drawer glide position in the cabinet by holding it tightly against the cabinet's front edge.

[11] Attach right-angle brackets to the top of the cabinet with ⅝" screws. These will be used to secure the worktop.

[12] Attach ½"-high by ¹¹⁄₁₆"-thick solid wood strips to all edges of the drawer faces. Use glue and brad nails to secure the strips. The nail holes can be hidden with wood filler.

TIP

As a general rule, drawers are made 1" smaller in width than the cabinet's inside dimension. File drawers need about 3" clearance above the drawer box, and utility drawers require a 1" space.

TIP

Drawer faces are normally 1" wider than the drawer opening width. In frameless-style cabinetry, drawer faces are usually spaced ¹⁄₁₆" apart. The bottom drawer face covers the bottom board edge, and the top drawer face is made to cover about ½" of the upper rail.

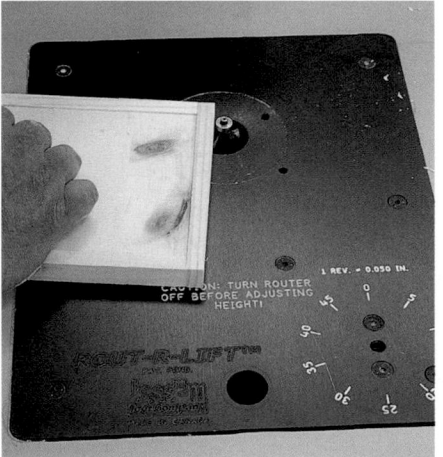

[13] Sand the wood strips smooth. Round over all four front edges of each face using a ⅜" roundover bit in a handheld router or in a table.

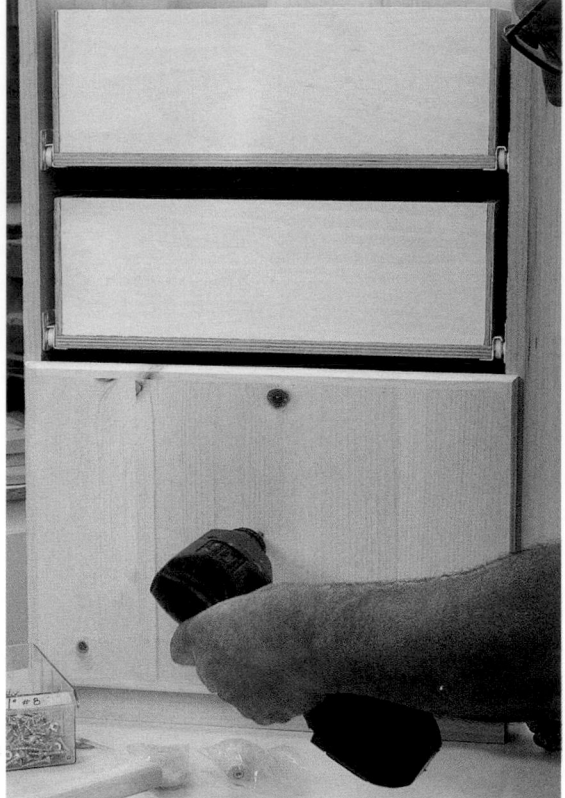

[14] The drawer faces can be easily and accurately located following a few simple steps. First purchase the handles or pulls that you plan to use. Drill the handle holes in the drawer faces only. Then use those screw holes to secure the face to the drawer box by driving 2" screws through the drawer face holes into the box. If you are satisfied with the drawer face location, drive two 1"-long screws through the backside of the front board into the drawer face. Remove the screws in the handle holes, drill completely through the drawer box and install the handles.

[Construction Notes]

These file and utility drawer modules can be made with any type of solid wood or sheet material. The frameless style is easy to build and relatively inexpensive when compared to the commercial versions. The full-back design makes this unit very sturdy and capable of supporting a great deal of weight.

Drawer sizes can be varied to suit your needs and combination-drawer, over-door or full-door modules with adjustable shelves can easily be designed and built. I have a 10' wood edge laminated top with four modules in my office, which provides me with separate computer and desk stations. There's a lot of storage for my files and office supplies, so it is an ideal work area.

Remember the basic height and spacing rules when building these modules. The only issue not discussed was cabinet depth. If you need a deeper cabinet to support a 30" or 36" top, increase the cabinet and drawer depths. Drawer glides are available in longer lengths to accommodate those deeper drawers.

My module was finished with three coats of polyurethane because it's a tough, hard finish. In a busy home office environment, a finish that can withstand some abuse is ideal.

[15] Install file-hanging hardware that is available at your local stationery store. Or you can use the shop-built technique that I will use in chapter ten (see step 16) to provide a track for the file hangers.

[16] Many other accessories are available for drawers. I purchased a pencil tray and installed an intermediate divider board to support the tray.

[chapter four]

desktop Organizer

If your desk is anything like mine, it's a cluttered mess. Vowing to resolve the situation, I designed this ultimate desk organizer. With slots for magazines, reference books and file folders, it's perfect for my cluttered ways! Two slide-out trays hold pens, paper clips, notes and checkbooks. The center bridge is great for CD storage. The light guard will shield a small fluorescent fixture I plan to install. The right side tower can hold mail or frequently used books. The locked center cabinet is the perfect place for documents that require secure storage.

In this project, there are a number of mortise-and-tenon joints to deal with; placement is critical. But if you're uncomfortable with this joinery, you could use simple butt joints and screws, biscuits or dowels. This project may appear complicated, but break it down into individual steps and you'll discover its simplicity.

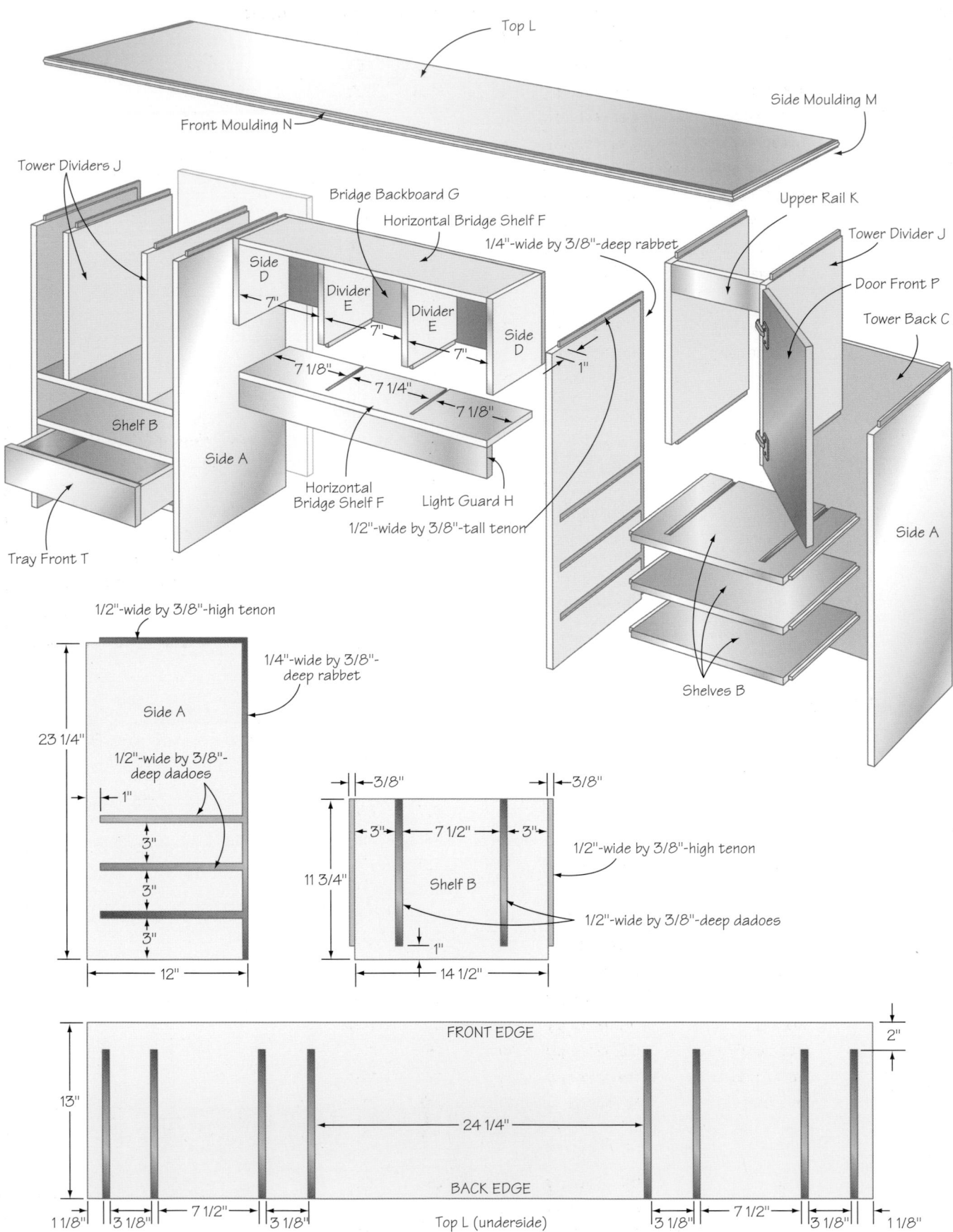

Top L

Side Moulding M

Front Moulding N

Tower Dividers J

Bridge Backboard G

Horizontal Bridge Shelf F

1/4"-wide by 3/8"-deep rabbet

Upper Rail K

Tower Divider J

Side
D

7"

Divider
E

7"

Divider
E

7"

Side
D

Door Front P

Tower Back C

1"

Shelf B

7 1/8"

7 1/4"

7 1/8"

Side A

Horizontal
Bridge Shelf F

Light Guard H

1/2"-wide by 3/8"-tall tenon

Side A

Tray Front T

Shelves B

1/2"-wide by 3/8"-high tenon

1/4"-wide by 3/8"-
deep rabbet

Side A

23 1/4"

1/2"-wide by 3/8"-
deep dadoes

1"

3"

3"

3"

12"

3/8"

3/8"

3"

7 1/2"

3"

11 3/4"

Shelf B

1/2"-wide by 3/8"-high tenon

1"

1/2"-wide by 3/8"-deep dadoes

14 1/2"

FRONT EDGE

2"

13"

24 1/4"

BACK EDGE

1 1/8"

3 1/8"

7 1/2"

3 1/8"

Top L (underside)

3 1/8"

7 1/2"

3 1/8"

1 1/8"

Cutting List • Desktop Organizer

REF.	QTY.	PART	MATERIAL	THICKNESS	WIDTH	LENGTH	COMMENTS
A	4	Sides	Oak veneer ply	¾	12	23⅝	
B	6	Horizontal shelves	Oak veneer ply	¾	11¾	15¼	
C	2	Tower backs	Oak veneer ply	¼	15¼	23⅝	
D	2	Bridge sides	Oak veneer ply	¾	7¾	7½	
E	2	Bridge dividers	Oak veneer ply	¾	7¾	6¾	
F	2	Horizontal bridge shelves	Oak veneer ply	¾	7¾	22½	
G	1	Bridge backboard	Oak veneer ply	¼	7½	24	
H	1	Light guard	Solid wood	¾	3½	24	
J	4	Tower dividers	Oak veneer ply	¾	13⅜	11¾	
K	1	Upper rail	Oak veneer ply	¾	1½	7½	
L	1	Top	Oak veneer ply	¾	13	58	
M	2	Side mouldings	Oak veneer ply	¾	¾	13⅜	
N	1	Front moulding	Oak veneer ply	¾	¾	58¾	
P	1	Door front	Solid wood	¾	8½	12½	

Pull-Out Trays

REF.	QTY.	PART	MATERIAL	THICKNESS	WIDTH	LENGTH	COMMENTS
Q	4	Sides	Baltic birch ply	½	2³⁄₁₆	11	
R	4	Backs and fronts	Baltic birch ply	½	2³⁄₁₆	13¹⁵⁄₁₆	
S	2	Bottoms	Baltic birch ply	½	11	14⁷⁄₁₆	
T	2	Tray fronts	Solid oak	¾	3½	15	

Hardware and Supplies

- Screws
- Nails
- Glue
- Biscuits or dowels
- 107° hidden hinges
- Commercial CD racks (optional)
- Door handles

Metric Cutting List • Desktop Organizer

REF.	QTY.	PART	MATERIAL	THICKNESS	WIDTH	LENGTH	COMMENTS
A	4	Sides	Oak veneer ply	19	305	600	
B	6	Horizontal shelves	Oak veneer ply	19	298	387	
C	2	Tower backs	Oak veneer ply	6	387	600	
D	2	Bridge sides	Oak veneer ply	19	197	191	
E	2	Bridge dividers	Oak veneer ply	19	197	171	
F	2	Horizontal bridge shelves	Oak veneer ply	19	197	572	
G	1	Bridge backboard	Oak veneer ply	6	191	610	
H	1	Light guard	Solid wood	19	89	610	
J	4	Tower dividers	Oak veneer ply	19	340	298	
K	1	Upper rail	Oak veneer ply	19	38	191	
L	1	Top	Oak veneer ply	19	330	1473	
M	2	Side mouldings	Oak veneer ply	19	19	340	
N	1	Front moulding	Oak veneer ply	19	19	1492	
P	1	Door front	Solid wood	19	216	318	

Pull-Out Trays

REF.	QTY.	PART	MATERIAL	THICKNESS	WIDTH	LENGTH	COMMENTS
Q	4	Sides	Baltic birch ply	13	56	279	
R	4	Backs and fronts	Baltic birch ply	13	56	354	
S	2	Bottoms	Baltic birch ply	13	279	367	
T	2	Tray fronts	Solid oak	19	89	381	

[1] Prepare the four sides (A) by applying wood veneer tape to the front (long) edge of each. As we did in other projects, use a flush-trim bit in a router to clean up the overhang on the edge tape.

[2] The four sides require three stopped dadoes, a stopped tenon and a rabbet cut. Follow the illustration for the cut locations. Use a router and ½"-wide straight bit for the dadoes and the table saw for the rabbets and tenons. All the dadoes, as well as the rabbet, are on the inside face of each sideboard. Be sure to orient the boards properly in pairs with the wood veneer edge to the front. The stopped tenon is on the top edge of each panel.

[3] Each side horizontal shelf (B) will have one 15¼" edge covered with veneer. This will be the front edge of each board. Both side edges require a tenon that's ½" thick and ⅜" deep on all the shelves. The tenons are stopped 1" short of the front edge. Round over the front corners of each tenon so they'll fit into the dadoes on the sideboards.

TIP

If you don't have a router or ½" bit, you can use butt joints, screws and glue. Adjust the panel sizes accordingly when eliminating the tenons.

[4] Two of the horizontal shelves (B) need two stopped dadoes on the top face. They will receive the vertical divider tenons in each tower. Cut the dadoes as detailed in the drawing, making sure they stop 1" short of the front edge.

[5] Cut the two backs (C) and assemble both towers. Use glue to secure the tenons in the dadoes and glue with brad nails to attach the backs. Leave both assemblies clamped until the adhesive sets.

[6] Cut the six panels for the bridge. Apply wood veneer tape to the front edge of each board. The two dividers (E) need a tenon ½" wide by ⅜" high on both top and bottom edges, stopped 1" short of the front edge. The horizontal shelves (F) need the corresponding stopped dado to receive the tenons.

[7] Assemble the bridge by first applying glue to secure the dividers. The end boards are attached with glue and 2" screws through the outside face of each panel into the horizontal shelf ends. To complete the bridge assembly, cut and install the backboard (G) with glue and brad nails.

[8] Attach the bridge to the two towers with glue and 1" screws driven through the tower side panels. Counterbore the screw holes and fill them with wood plugs before installing the tower dividers. The bridge is aligned with the back side of each tower and level with the bottom of each side tenon.

[9] The light guard is made from solid wood and has the bottom front edge rounded over with a ⅜" router bit. Secure the guard to the bottom of the bridge, flush with the front edge of the bottom board, using glue and biscuits. Drive a 2"-long finishing nail through the inside of each tower side and into the light guard end to further secure this board.

[10] Cut the four tower dividers (J) and apply wood veneer tape to the front edge on each board. Form a stopped tenon that's ½" wide by ⅜" high, centered on the top and bottom edge, of each divider. As with all the other tenons, cut them 1" short of the front edge on each panel. Install the dividers with glue on the tenons and nails driven through the backboard. Take care to align the dividers properly.

[11] The section where a door will be installed in the right side tower requires an upper rail. Use ¾" plywood veneer with a taped bottom edge, or use a solid piece of wood. Apply glue to the ends and clamp the rail flush with the top edges of dividers. This rail is needed to provide door-to-top board clearance.

[12] The top board requires matching dadoes to accept the eight tenons. Each dado must be ½" wide by ⅜" deep and stopped 1" short of the front edge. Use the drawing as a guide to find the dado placement. However, the best method is to lay the top board in place and mark the dado positions. After cutting the top board (L) to size, form a stopped rabbet on the back underside face. The rabbet is ¼" wide by ⅜" deep and stopped 1" short at both ends. Apply glue to the tenons as well as on top of the bridge and clamp the top in place. Use brad nails to secure the backboards.

[13] Select a suitable moulding that's ¾" high and attach to the front and two sides of the top board. Use glue and brad nails to secure the strips. Miter the corners at 45°. Once again, use the measurements in the cutting list as a guide. It's good practice to confirm the dimensions on your project.

[14] Build two pull-out trays using the dimensions listed. Each tray side (Q) requires a ½"-wide by ¼"-deep rabbet on both ends to accept the front and back boards. Assemble the tray box with glue and brad nails. Cut the bottom board accurately as it will force the box into square when installed.

[15] The two tray fronts are solid wood pieces with the front face rounded over. Use a ⅜" roundover bit in a router to ease the edges. Secure the fronts to each tray box with 1" screws driven through the front board and into the backside of the tray front.

[16] The right side tower door is solid wood and mounted with 107° full-overlay hidden hinges. See chapter five for door-mounting instructions. I've also installed a small barrel lock on this door. These locks are simple to install and are available in most home centers.

[Construction Notes]

I used a spray lacquer to finish my organizer. Getting a paintbrush into all the small compartments would have been messy and time-consuming. There are hundreds of finishes available in spray cans so you should be able to match the desk finish where the organizer will be installed.

Once again, I built this project using my favorite multi-core veneer board. However, any sheet material such as wood veneer plywood or wood veneer PB can be used. If the organizer is going to be finished with a solid color, consider MDF as an alternative. MDF is relatively inexpensive and is easily machined.

Don't get discouraged by the number of dadoes and tenons for this project. If you don't have the equipment or experience, use butt joints, glue and screws. In my opinion, it's perfectly acceptable.

As always, I've detailed a project with panel positions and features to suit my requirements. If the placement of these section panels doesn't meet your needs, change them accordingly. Everyone has special storage problems, so build a unit that functions for you.

The bridge section determines the overall width of the organizer. Its dimension is variable. If your desk isn't 60" wide, change the bridge dimensions. That is also true of the overall width for the organizer and it is easily modified to your situation.

chapter five

basic Workstation

This simple workstation consists of a file/storage drawer module tower, laminate desktop, bookcase end and a simple hutch. It's built using decorative joinery screws that allow for disassembly. You could use standard biscuit or screw-and-glue joinery, but if you have, say, a college student who is always moving, joinery screws are the answer.

Since computers now play such a large role in our work and school activities, I've included a raised, closed stand attached to the back of the bookcase for the stor-age of a computer CPU. The desktop is designed so the computer monitor can be placed on the right side. The desk area in front of the chair can be used for paperwork. A commercially available pull-out keyboard tray also can be attached underneath the desktop, directly in front of the seat space.

The file/storage tower has three utility drawers and a large capacity cabinet for paper storage. The tower top is an ideal place for a printer — it's out of the way but still easily accessible.

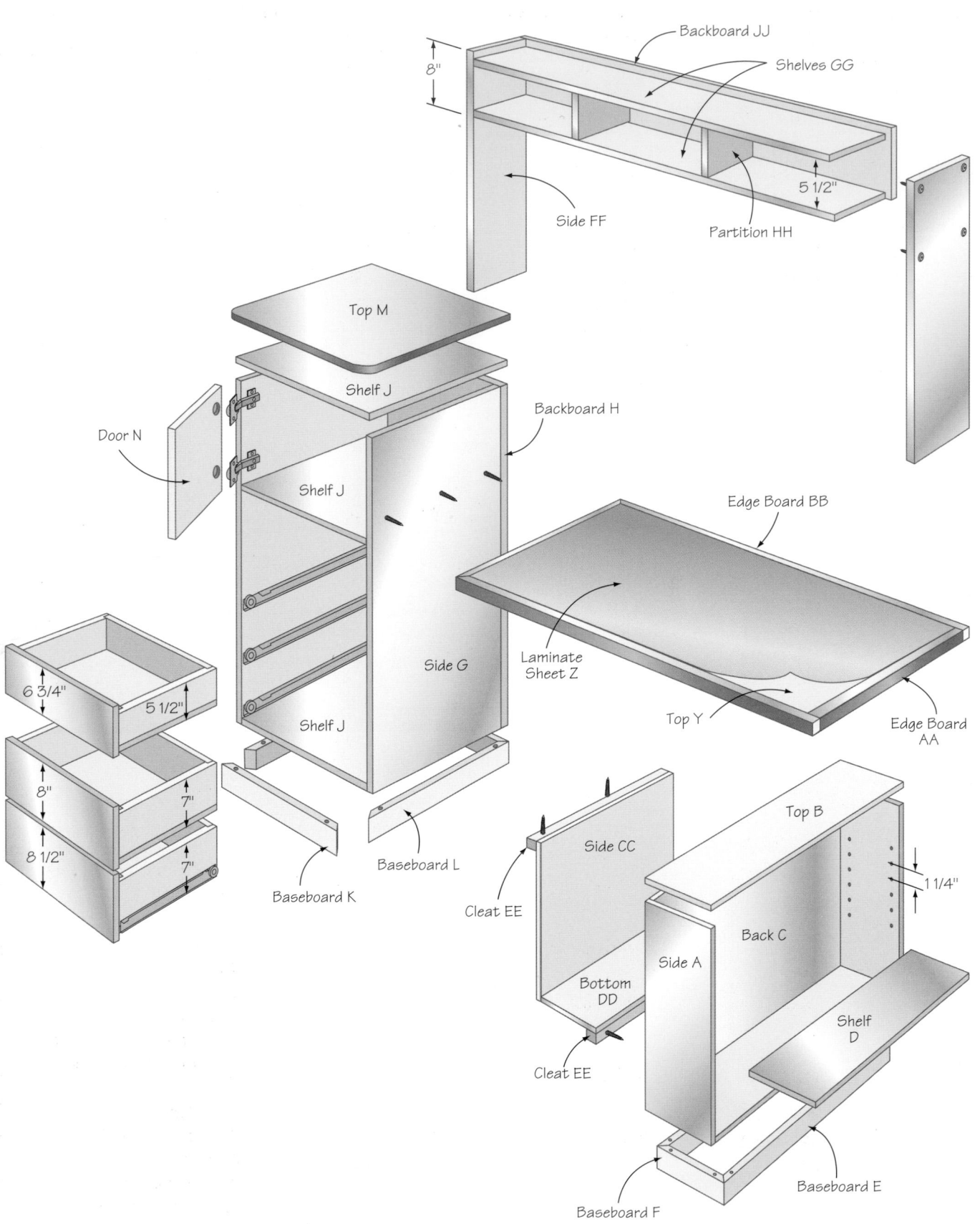

Backboard JJ

Shelves GG

8"

Side FF

Partition HH

5 1/2"

Top M

Shelf J

Backboard H

Door N

Shelf J

Edge Board BB

6 3/4"

5 1/2"

Shelf J

Side G

Laminate
Sheet Z

Top Y

Edge Board
AA

8"

7"

8 1/2"

7"

Shelf J

Baseboard L

Baseboard K

Top B

Side CC

1 1/4"

Cleat EE

Side A

Back C

Bottom
DD

Shelf
D

Cleat EE

Baseboard E

Baseboard F

Cutting List • Basic Workstation

REF.	QTY.	PART	MATERIAL	THICKNESS	WIDTH	LENGTH	COMMENTS
A	2	Sides	Veneer PB	11/16	10	27 3/4	
B	2	Bottom and top	Veneer PB	11/16	10	23 1/2	
C	1	Back	Veneer PB	11/16	23 1/2	26 3/8	
D	2	Shelves	Veneer PB	11/16	9 1/4	23 7/16	
E	2	Baseboards	Solid wood	3/4	1 1/2	23	
F	2	Baseboards	Solid wood	3/4	1 1/2	8	
Printer Tower							
G	2	Side panels	Veneer PB	11/16	21 3/4	36 1/2	
H	1	Backboard	Veneer PB	11/16	18	36 1/2	
J	3	Fixed shelves	Veneer PB	11/16	16 5/8	21 3/4	
K	2	Baseboards	Solid wood	3/4	1 1/2	16	
L	2	Baseboards	Solid wood	3/4	1 1/2	20 1/2	
M	1	Top	Veneer PB	11/16	18	23 1/2	
N	1	Door	Veneer PB	11/16	12 1/4	17 5/8	
Drawers & Drawer Fronts							
P	4	Sides	Birch ply	1/2	6 1/2	18	
Q	4	Front and back	Birch ply	1/2	6 1/2	15 1/8	
R	2	Bottoms	Birch ply	1/2	15 5/8	18	
S	2	Sides	Birch ply	1/2	5	18	
T	2	Front and back	Birch ply	1/2	5	15 1/8	
U	1	Bottom	Birch ply	1/2	15 5/8	18	
V	1	Bottom drawer front	Veneer PB	11/16	8 1/2	17 5/8	
W	1	Middle drawer front	Veneer PB	11/16	8	17 5/8	
X	1	Top drawer front	Veneer PB	11/16	6 3/4	17 5/8	
Desktop							
Y	1	Top	PB	3/4	25	50	
Z	1	Laminate sheet		N/A	27	52	GP grade
AA	2	Edge boards	Solid wood	3/4	1 1/2	25	
BB	2	Edge boards	Solid wood	3/4	1 1/2	51 1/2	
CPU Compartment							
CC	1	Side	Veneer PB	11/16	19	19	
DD	1	Bottom	Veneer PB	11/16	10	19	
EE	2	Cleats	Solid wood	3/4	1 1/2	18	
Hutch							
FF	2	Sides	Veneer PB	11/16	7	29 1/2	
GG	2	Horizontal shelf	Veneer PB	11/16	7	47 5/8	
HH	2	Vertical partition	Veneer PB	11/16	5 1/2	7	
JJ	1	Backboard	Veneer PB	11/16	8	49	

Hardware and Supplies

- Veneer edge
- Tape
- Screws
- Nails
- Glue
- Biscuits or dowels
- Three-quarter extension drawer glides
- Full-extension drawer glides for the file drawer
- 107° hidden hinges
- High-pressure laminate
- Contact cement
- Cable hole grommets
- Commercial CD racks (optional)
- Pull-out keyboard tray
- Drawer handles

Metric Cutting List • Basic Workstation

REF.	QTY.	PART	MATERIAL	THICKNESS	WIDTH	LENGTH	COMMENTS
A	2	Sides	Veneer PB	18	254	10	
B	2	Bottom and top	Veneer PB	18	254	10	
C	1	Back	Veneer PB	18	597	10	
D	2	Shelves	Veneer PB	18	235	10	
E	2	Baseboards	Solid wood	19	38	23	
F	2	Baseboards	Solid wood	19	38	8	
Printer Tower							
G	2	Side panels	Veneer PB	18	552	3	
H	1	Backboard	Veneer PB	18	457	36	
J	3	Fixed shelves	Veneer PB	18	422	21	
K	2	Baseboards	Solid wood	19	38	16	
L	2	Baseboards	Solid wood	19	38	20	
M	1	Top	Veneer PB	18	457	23	
N	1	Door	Veneer PB	18	311	17	
Drawers & Drawer Fronts							
P	4	Sides	Birch ply	13	165	18	
Q	4	Front and back	Birch ply	13	165	15	
R	2	Bottoms	Birch ply	13	397	18	
S	2	Sides	Birch ply	13	127	18	
T	2	Front and back	Birch ply	13	127	15	
U	1	Bottom	Birch ply	13	397	18	
V	1	Bottom drawer front	Veneer PB	18	216	17	
W	1	Middle drawer front	Veneer PB	18	203	17	
X	1	Top drawer front	Veneer PB	18	171	17	
Desktop							
Y	1	Top	PB	19	635	50	
Z	1	Laminate sheet		N/A	686	52	GP grade
AA	2	Edge boards	Solid wood	19	38	25	
BB	2	Edge boards	Solid wood	19	38	51	
CPU Compartment							
CC	1	Side	Veneer PB	18	483	483	
DD	1	Bottom	Veneer PB	18	254	483	
EE	2	Cleats	Solid wood	19	38	457	
Hutch							
FF	2	Sides	Veneer PB	18	178	29	
GG	2	Horizontal shelf	Veneer PB	18	178	47	
HH	2	Vertical partition	Veneer PB	18	140	7	
JJ	1	Backboard	Veneer PB	18	203	49	

[1] Cut the two sides (A), and the top and bottom boards (B). Apply iron-on wood veneer edge tape to one long side on each of the four boards.

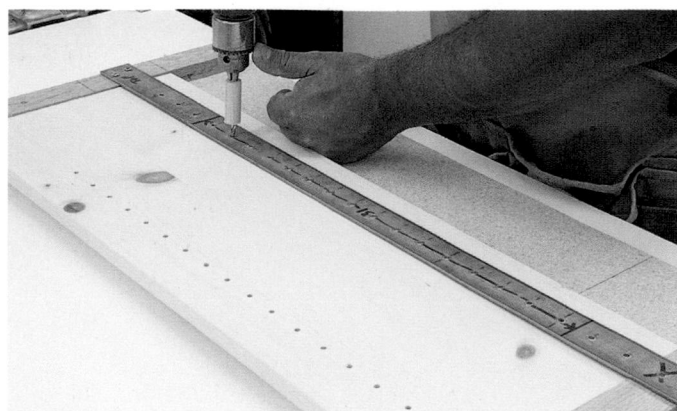

[2] Drill holes on the inside face of each side panel for the adjustable shelf pins. You can make a simple jig such as the one shown in the photograph or mark the holes and use a drill press. I spaced my holes 1¼" apart but any spacing is acceptable.

[3] The sides are joined to the top and bottom boards. The joint can be made using glue in combination with biscuits, dowels or screws. I have decided to use only decorative assembly screws for easy dismantling and transportation. This type of hardware comes in many forms, such as the big cap screws I'm using, as well as screws with washers. Be sure the hardware you use is designed for PB joinery if that's the material you plan to use. And, always drill the proper size pilot hole for that fastener to achieve maximum hold.

[4] Install the inset back with two screws on each edge. Its back face should be set flush with the back edge of the top, bottom and side boards.

[5] Join the four baseboards with 45° angled cuts at each corner. Use glue and nails to secure the four joints. The outside dimension of the base frame should be 8" deep by 23" long. Attach the frame to the bottom board of the bookcase with 1½"-long screws in counterbored holes. The base frame is attached so it's equally spaced on all four sides.

TIP

Wood veneer edge tape comes in a number of widths and lengths. The simplest type to apply is the pre-glued material that is heat activated with an iron. I'm using pine veneer, which trims cleanly with a double-edged trimmer. However, wide-grained woods such as oak should be trimmed with a flush-trim bit in a router.

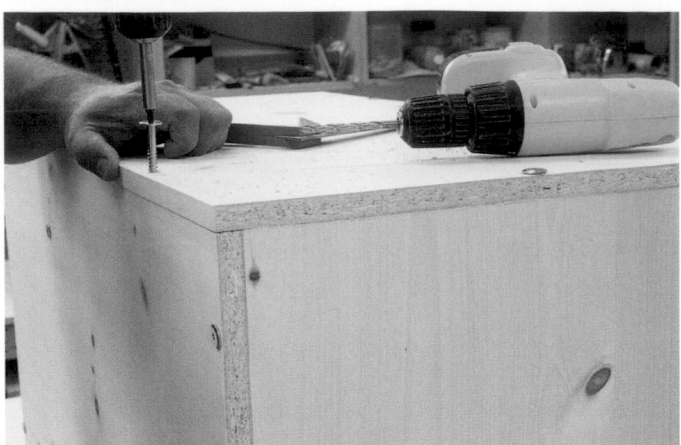

[6] Cut the two adjustable shelf boards (D). Apply wood veneer to one long edge on each board. Then prepare the two side panels (G) and the three fixed shelves (J) by applying wood veneer edge tape to one long edge on each side board and one short edge on each of the fixed shelves. The top fixed shelf is installed flush with the top end of the side boards as shown here, and the bottom fixed shelf with the bottom ends. The middle fixed shelf is attached so its top surface is 24" from the bottom ends of each side panel.

[7] Apply wood veneer tape to both long edges of the backboard. Secure the backboard to the cabinet so its edges are flush with the top, bottom and both side boards.

[8] Join the four baseboards with 45° angled cuts at each corner. Use glue and nails to secure the four joints. The outside dimension of the base frame should be 16" wide by 20½" deep. Attach the frame to the bottom board of the printer tower with 1½"-long screws in counterbored holes. The base frame is attached so it's equally spaced on all four sides.

[9] The printer tower top is made from ¹¹⁄₁₆"-thick veneer PB and wood veneer edge tape. Slightly round the front corners of the top with a belt sander. Apply the wood veneer tape with a hot iron. The heat will soften the veneer tape, allowing it to be formed around each front corner, creating a seamless band on the front and two side edges. Then align the top flush with the cabinet back and both side boards. It will overhang in front by 1¹⁄₁₆". Use four 1¼"-long screws to secure the top from inside the cabinet.

[10] Cut all the drawer parts to size following the dimensions given in the cutting list. Refer to chapter three for drawer-building procedures.

[12] The door is made from 11/16"-thick veneer PB. All four edges must have veneer tape applied. Two 35mm holes must be drilled in the door to accept the hidden hinges. They are usually placed 4" from each end and 3/16" back from the door edge. A hinge-boring bit in a drill press is the best way to form these holes.

To install these hinges perfectly every time, first secure the hinges to the door with their mounting plates attached (use a square to align the hinges at right angles to the door edge). Next, hold the door in its normally open position with a 1/8"-thick spacing stick between the door edge and cabinet face. Drive 5/8"-long screws through the hinge plate and into the cabinet side on both hinges. Once each hinge plate is secured with two screws, detach the hinge from its plate and install the remaining screws. Attach the door and adjust if necessary. I'm using two 107° Blum full-overlay hinges on my door.

[11] Cut the three drawer faces to size as shown in the cutting list. Apply wood veneer edge tape to all the face edges. Install the three drawer faces with a 1/16" space between each. The bottom face is flush with the underside of the bottom fixed shelf. Refer to chapter three for installation tips.

[Calculating Door Widths]

You can easily calculate the exact width of the door or doors you'll need when using full-overlay hidden hinges. Add 1" to the inside width of the cabinet. That will be your required door size. If you need two doors, simply divide that number by two. For example, a 24"-wide frameless-style cabinet, built with 5/8"-thick sheet goods, has an inside dimension of 22¾" (24" minus the thickness of both sides). By applying the 1" rule, I'll need one door 23¾" wide or two doors each 11⅞" wide.

The same rule is used for face-frame cabinets as well. Remember to measure the smallest inside dimension. In the case of face-frame cabinets, the dimension is taken from inside stile (vertical face-frame member) face to inside stile face. Then, add 1" and divide by 2 if you need two doors.

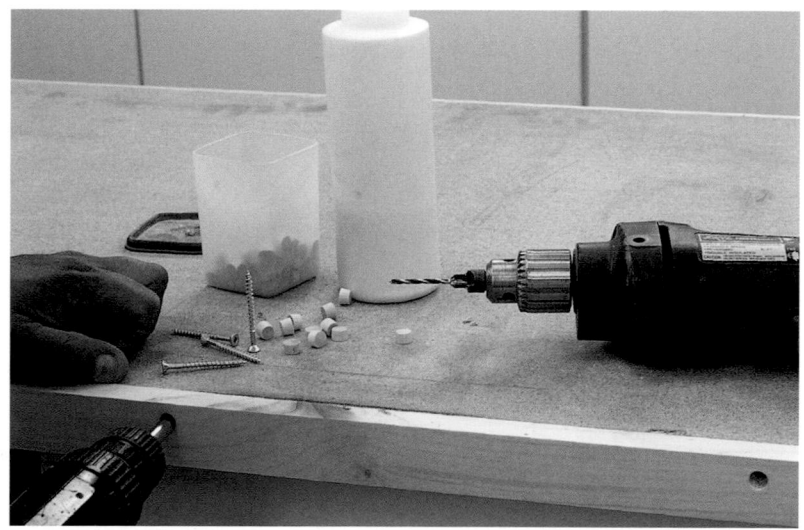

[13] Build the laminate wood-edge desktop following the instructions detailed in chapter two. Use the dimensions shown in the cutting list for this project.

[14] Attach the top to the bookcase end with three 1¼"-long screws. Secure the other end to the printer tower side with screws through the inside of the cabinet. Verify that the top is level. The top surface should be 30½₆" above the floor.

[15] The CPU stand is built using ¹¹⁄₁₆" edge-taped veneer PB and two solid wood cleats. Use three screws to attach the boards, and secure the cleats with glue and screws. The cleats should have the outside corners rounded over with a belt sander to avoid injuries if someone bumps against them. One cleat is attached on the top outside face and the other on the bottom board's outside edge.

[16] Secure the CPU shelf to the backside of the bookcase and underside of the desktop. Use three 1¼"-long screws through each cleat.

[17] Prepare the hutch boards by applying wood veneer edge tape to all front and top edges. Tape all the edges on the backboard, as they will be visible. Secure the sides to horizontal shelves using decorative screws. The lower horizontal shelf's bottom edge should be 8" below each side's top edge. The upper shelf will be 5½" above to leave the proper clearance for both vertical dividers. The backboard is attached flush with the underside of the lower horizontal shelf and even with the sides' top edges. All of the boards can be installed with decorative screws. Divide the shelf into three equal spaces and install the vertical dividers. The hutch can be attached to the tower side with screws through the underside of the desktop on the right-hand side.

[18] A commercial plastic pull-out tray is the simplest solution for the keyboard. They're inexpensive, rugged and easy to install. You can also purchase hole grommets for the monitor cables.

[chapter six]

executive Work Center

The unique, but simple to build, executive work center has a few hidden design options that will suit almost anyone's needs. The frame-and-panel-style desk has wood compartments that can be fully customized. If you prefer a file drawer in place of the computer processing unit (CPU) cabinet, simply build a different sized box to attach to the desk. The basic desk style remains even though the drawer or door compartments are different.

I've used solid wood legs, ¾"-thick veneer plywood and a solid wood glued-up top. I've also opted to use a full ¾"-thick back on the hutch as well as all the panels. It's a little more expensive, but it's money well invested.

The panel to leg joints give this desk added strength and durability. The full ¾"-thick grooves provide more glue surface and are further strengthened with 2" wood screws.

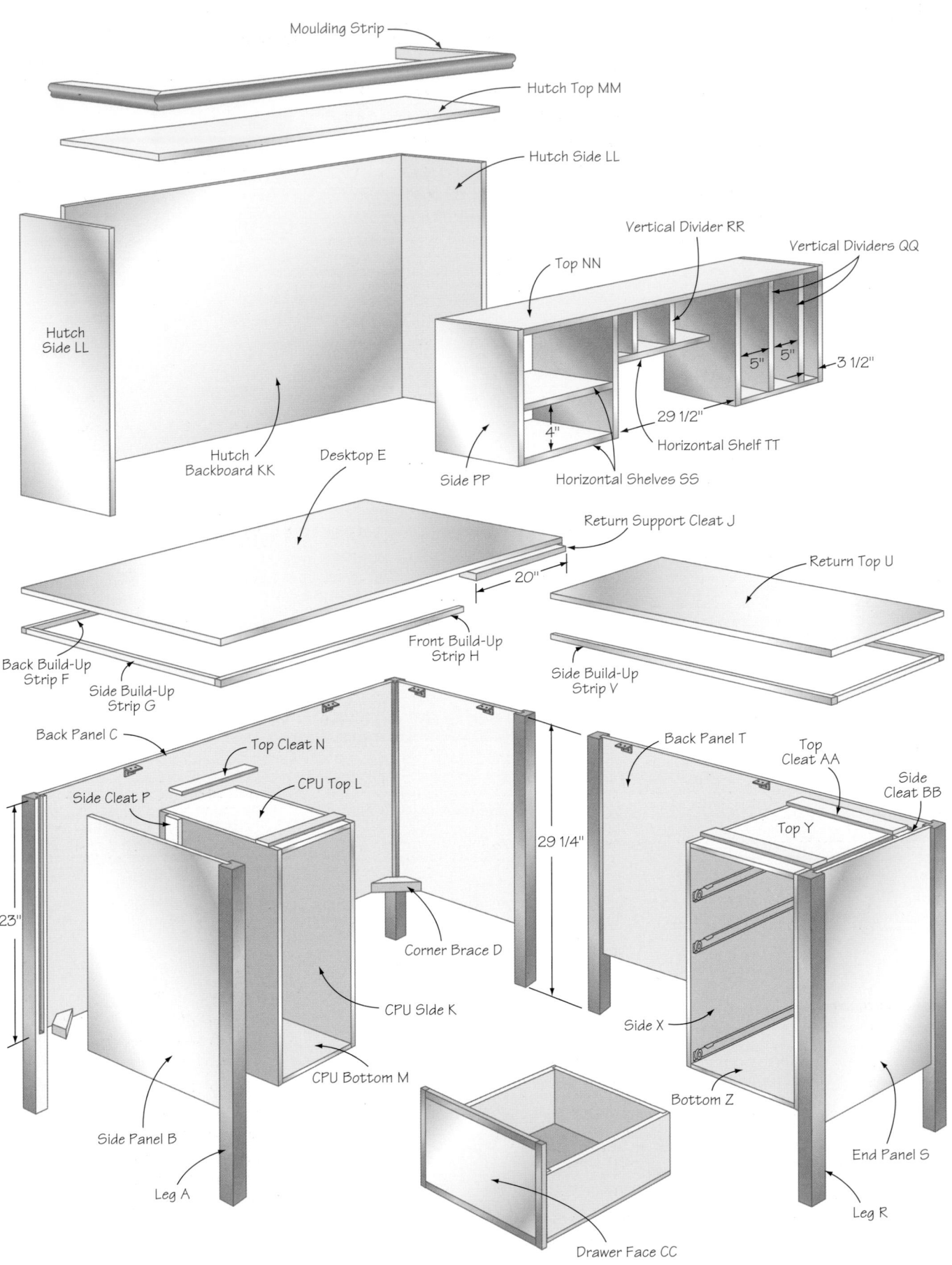

Moulding Strip

Hutch Top MM

Hutch Side LL

Vertical Divider RR

Vertical Dividers QQ

Top NN

Hutch
Side LL

5" 5"

3 1/2"

29 1/2"

Horizontal Shelf TT

4"

Hutch
Backboard KK

Desktop E

Side PP

Horizontal Shelves SS

Return Support Cleat J

Return Top U

20"

Back Build-Up
Strip F

Side Build-Up
Strip G

Front Build-Up
Strip H

Side Build-Up
Strip V

Back Panel C

Top Cleat N

CPU Top L

Back Panel T

Top
Cleat AA

Side
Cleat BB

Side Cleat P

Top Y

29 1/4"

Corner Brace D

CPU Slde K

Side X

23"

CPU Bottom M

Bottom Z

Side Panel B

End Panel S

Leg A

Drawer Face CC

Leg R

Cutting List • Executive Work Center

REF.	QTY.	PART	MATERIAL	THICK	WIDTH	LENGTH	COMMENTS
A	4	Desk legs	Solid oak	1⅝	1⅝	29¼	
B	2	Desk side panels	Oak veneer ply	¾	23	25½	
C	1	Desk back panel	Oak veneer ply	¾	23	61½	
D	2	Rear corner braces	Solid oak	1⅝	1⅝	8	
E	1	Desktop	Solid oak	¾	30	66	Make from glued-up boards
F	1	Back build-up strip	Solid oak	¾	¾	64½	
G	2	Side build-up strips	Solid oak	¾	¾	30	
H	1	Front build-up strip	Solid oak	¾	¾	44½	
J	1	Return support cleat	Solid oak	¾	1½	20	
K	2	CPU sides	Oak veneer ply	¾	18	21	
L	1	CPU top	Oak veneer ply	¾	18	12	
M	1	CPU bottom	Oak veneer ply	¾	18	12	
N	2	CPU top cleats	Oak veneer ply	¾	1½	13	
P	1	CPU side cleat	Oak veneer ply	⅜	1½	21	
Q	1	CPU door	Oak veneer ply	¾	13	20⅞	Edged with solid ½"-thick wood strips
R	3	Return legs	Solid oak	1⅝	1⅝	29¼	
S	1	Return end panels	Oak veneer ply	¾	23	17	
T	1	Return back panel	Oak veneer ply	¾	23	37½	
U	1	Return top	Solid oak	¾	21½	42	Make from glued-up boards
V	2	Side build-up strips	Solid oak	¾	¾	42	
W	1	End build-up strip	Solid oak	¾	¾	20	

Drawer Compartment & Drawers

REF.	QTY.	PART	MATERIAL	THICK	WIDTH	LENGTH	COMMENTS
X	2	Compartment sides	Oak veneer ply	¾	18	21	
Y	1	Compartment top	Oak veneer ply	¾	18	10	
Z	1	Compartment bottom	Oak veneer ply	¾	18	10	
AA	2	Top cleats	Oak veneer ply	¾	1½	11½	
BB	1	Side cleat	Oak veneer ply	⅜	1½	21	
CC	3	Drawer faces	Oak veneer ply	¾	6⅞	11	Edged with solid ½"-thick wood strips
DD	4	Drawer sides	Baltic birch ply	½	5½	18	
EE	4	Drawer backs & fronts	Baltic birch ply	½	5½	8½	
FF	2	Drawer bottoms	Baltic birch ply	½	9	18	
GG	2	Top drawer sides	Baltic birch ply	½	4½	18	
HH	2	Top drw. backs & fronts	Baltic birch ply	½	4½	18	
JJ	1	Top drawer bottom	Baltic birch ply	½	9	18	

Hutch & Hutch Divider

REF.	QTY.	PART	MATERIAL	THICK	WIDTH	LENGTH	COMMENTS
KK	1	Backboard	Oak veneer ply	¾	28	64	
LL	2	Sides	Oak veneer ply	¾	11	28	
MM	1	Top board	Oak veneer ply	¾	11¾	64	
NN	1	Hutch divider top	Oak veneer ply	¾	11	62½	
PP	4	Vertical sides	Oak veneer ply	¾	11	12	
QQ	2	Vertical dividers	Oak veneer ply	¾	11	11¼	
RR	2	Vertical dividers	Oak veneer ply	¾	6	6	
SS	3	Horizontal shelves	Oak veneer ply	¾	11	15	
TT	1	Horizontal shelf	Oak veneer ply	¾	6	29½	

Hardware and Supplies

Veneer edge
Tape
Screws
Nails
Glue
Biscuits or dowels
Three-quarter extension drawer glides
Full-extension drawer glides for the file drawer
107° hidden hinges
High-pressure laminate
Contact cement
Cable hole grommets
Commercial CD racks (optional)
Pull-out keyboard tray
Drawer and door handles
Metal brackets

Metric Cutting List • Executive Work Center

REF.	QTY.	PART	MATERIAL	THICK	WIDTH	LENGTH	COMMENTS
A	4	Desk legs	Solid oak	41	41	743	
B	2	Desk side panels	Oak veneer ply	19	584	648	
C	1	Desk back panel	Oak veneer ply	19	584	1562	
D	2	Rear corner braces	Solid oak	41	41	203	
E	1	Desktop	Solid oak	19	762	1676	Make from glued-up boards
F	1	Back build-up strip	Solid oak	19	19	1639	
G	2	Side build-up strips	Solid oak	19	19	762	
H	1	Front build-up strip	Solid oak	19	19	1131	
J	1	Return support cleat	Solid oak	19	38	508	
K	2	CPU sides	Oak veneer ply	19	457	533	
L	1	CPU top	Oak veneer ply	19	457	305	
M	1	CPU bottom	Oak veneer ply	19	457	305	
N	2	CPU top cleats	Oak veneer ply	19	38	330	
P	1	CPU side cleat	Oak veneer ply	10	38	533	
Q	1	CPU door	Oak veneer ply	19	330	530	Edged with solid 13mm-thick wood strips
R	3	Return legs	Solid oak	41	41	743	
S	1	Return end panels	Oak veneer ply	19	584	432	
T	1	Return back panel	Oak veneer ply	19	584	953	
U	1	Return top	Solid oak	19	546	1067	Make from glued-up boards
V	2	Side build-up strips	Solid oak	19	19	1067	
W	1	End build-up strip	Solid oak	19	19	508	

Drawer Compartment & Drawers

REF.	QTY.	PART	MATERIAL	THICK	WIDTH	LENGTH	COMMENTS
X	2	Compartment sides	Oak veneer ply	19	457	533	
Y	1	Compartment top	Oak veneer ply	19	457	254	
Z	1	Compartment bottom	Oak veneer ply	19	457	254	
AA	2	Top cleats	Oak veneer ply	19	38	292	
BB	1	Side cleat	Oak veneer ply	10	38	533	
CC	3	Drawer faces	Oak veneer ply	19	174	279	Edged with solid 13mm-thick wood strips
DD	4	Drawer sides	Baltic birch ply	13	140	457	
EE	4	Drawer backs & fronts	Baltic birch ply	13	140	216	
FF	2	Drawer bottoms	Baltic birch ply	13	229	457	
GG	2	Top drawer sides	Baltic birch ply	13	115	457	
HH	2	Top drw. backs & fronts	Baltic birch ply	13	115	457	
JJ	1	Top drawer bottom	Baltic birch ply	13	229	457	

Hutch & Hutch Divider

REF.	QTY.	PART	MATERIAL	THICK	WIDTH	LENGTH	COMMENTS
KK	1	Backboard	Oak veneer ply	19	711	1626	
LL	2	Sides	Oak veneer ply	19	279	711	
MM	1	Top board	Oak veneer ply	19	298	1626	
NN	1	Hutch divider top	Oak veneer ply	19	279	1588	
PP	4	Vertical sides	Oak veneer ply	19	279	305	
QQ	2	Vertical dividers	Oak veneer ply	19	279	285	
RR	2	Vertical dividers	Oak veneer ply	19	152	152	
SS	3	Horizontal shelves	Oak veneer ply	19	279	381	
TT	1	Horizontal shelf	Oak veneer ply	19	152	750	

[1] Cut the four legs of the desk to size. Two of the legs require a groove that's ¾"-wide by ⅜"-deep by 23"-long on one face measured from the top of the legs. The other two require two grooves of the same size on two adjoining faces of each leg. All the grooves are centered on the leg faces. The grooves are formed with a ¾"-wide straight router bit on a router table. The cut will have a rounded bottom requiring each to be squared so the panels will fit properly.

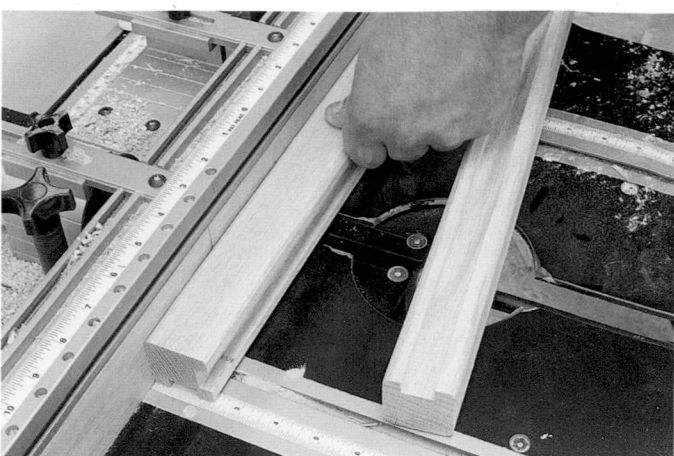

[2] Use a ⅜" roundover bit in a router table to soften the vertical edges on all of the legs. Now is an ideal time to complete the sanding on the legs as the task will be much more difficult after the panels are installed.

[3] Attach the side panels to the legs. One double-grooved back leg is at the end of each side panel. Be careful to orient the legs properly so they will receive the back panel. Secure the panels using glue and 2" screws in counterbored holes (they will be filled with wood plugs, through the side opposite each panel edge). Position the screws 2" from the bottom and top edge of each panel.

> **TIP**
>
> *The legs for the desk and return are prepared in the same manner. Also, note that the panels for both pieces are the same height. To save time and eliminate duplicate set-ups, cut the desk and return legs, as well as the panels, at the same time.*

[4] Install the back panel joining the two desk side assemblies. The panel is secured in the second groove on each back leg and held with glue and screws. Insert these screws, through the leg face opposite the end edges, 2½" from the top and bottom of the back panel on both ends.

> **TIP**
>
> *Always drill a pilot hole for the screw. The screw will cut threads for maximum hold. Without pilot holes the screw shaft is acting like a wedge and could split the material.*

[5] The two rear corner braces are attached with glue and screws in plugged holes. Before cutting the 45° angle on each end, round over all the edges with a ⅜" bit in a router. Align the sides to the back board at 90° with a carpenter's square before securing the braces. Use 1½"-long screws.

[6] Join enough solid wood boards to form a top that measures ¾"-thick by 30"-deep by 66"-wide. Joint the edges and use biscuits to create the top. I am using six 1x6 boards to build my top, with biscuits 6" apart.

TIP

You can create acceptable edges for joining without a jointer. The straight edges can be cut on a table saw as long as the saw is properly aligned. Use the factory edge and cut the opposite side, reducing the width by 1/16". Reverse the board so the cut edge is against the saw fence, and cut another 1/16" off the opposite side. It may be necessary to make more than two cuts but you will achieve an edge that can be joined providing the saw is well-tuned and accurately aligned. Or, if you don't have a biscuit cutter, simple edge-to-edge gluing will also yield an acceptable result. Don't over-tighten the clamps as this will force all the glue out and starve the joint.

[7] Attach right-angle metal brackets every 6" along the back and two sides of the desk frame. These will be used to secure the top.

[8] Once the glued-up top is properly set, trim it to the correct finished size. Install ¾" square build-up strips on the underside, as detailed in the drawing, with glue and finishing nails. The strips are installed flush with the outside edges of the desktop. The edge will be rounded over once the return is attached.

[9] Attach the top to the desk base using ⅝" screws through the angle brackets. The top should overhang the legs by 1" on all faces. Don't glue the top in place. This will allow it to move a little during humidity level changes.

TIP

A situation called "bridging" can occur when joining two boards with screws. The threads will run to their ends before both boards are joined tightly leaving a gap in between both. To eliminate this problem, drill a hole larger than the screw diameter in the piece closest to the screw head. The screw will simply rotate in that piece without creating a thread and draw the pieces tightly together. You'll always get tight joints using this technique. Drill larger holes in the return cleat to avoid bridging between the cleat and tops.

[10] Cut and install the return support cleat. It should extend ¾" past the front edge of the desktop. Use 1¼" screws to secure the cleat.

[11] Apply iron-on wood veneer edge tape to all four front edges of the CPU compartment boards. Join the two sides (K) to the top and bottom boards (L and M) as shown in the illustration. Use glue and 2" screws in counterbored holes that are filled with wood plugs.

[12] Attach the two top cleats on the CPU compartment with glue and finishing nails. The side cleat is ⅜" thick and will fill the gap between the desk leg and side panel. Secure it with glue and finishing nails on the rear left side of the compartment.

[13] Install the CPU compartment, aligning its front edge flush with the face of the desk leg. Use 2"-long screws into the leg, 1 ½" screws at the back into the side panel, and 2" screws through the top of the compartment into the underside of the desktop. Locate the front screws, which are driven into the leg, 4" on center from the top and bottom of the compartment. The mounting plate of the door hinge will hide them.

[14] Cut a piece of ¾" veneer plywood measuring 12" x 19⅞". Glue and nail ¾"-thick by ½"-high hardwood strips to all edges. Finally, sand and round over the front face edges with a ⅜" router bit. Note: The door for the CPU compartment is made with ¾" veneer plywood and hardwood edge strips. The door width is found by measuring the inside dimension of the compartment and adding 1". The inside dimension is 12", therefore our door width must be 13". The door height for this application covers the top and bottom board edges less ⅛" for desktop clearance. Our finished height is 20⅞". These rules apply when using full-overlay hidden hinges.

[15] Drill two 35mm holes on the back of the door that are 4" on center from the top and bottom edges. Install two 110° full-overlay hidden hinges in the holes with the mounting plates attached. Use a ⅛"-thick spacer between the door edge, in its normally open position, and the compartment edge. Hold the door flush with the underside surface of the bottom board and drive screws into the mounting plates (this technique will accurately locate your door).

[16] Cut the three return legs, and form one groove in two of the legs and two on the third leg. Follow the same procedures as detailed in step one for the desk legs. Cut the side and rear return panels and attach them in the same way the desk panels were installed.

[17] The solid wood return top is made following the same steps performed during the desktop construction. However, its finished size is 21½" deep by 42" long.

[18] Attach ¾" square build-up strips to the underside of the return top. These are again installed with glue and nails. The return end with one leg is left open so it can be secured to the return cleat on the desk.

[19] The top is attached to the return base with right-angle brackets. Then, the return is connected to the desk with screws through the return cleat. Sand the tops smooth and round over the five outside corners to prevent injury. Use a small round object about 1½" in diameter to form identical arcs on each corner. Next, soften the sharp corners with a belt sander.

[20] Use a ⅜" roundover bit in a router to remove the sharp edges on both the desk and return top. Round over the bottom and top edges.

[21] Build the drawer compartment following the same procedures as detailed for the CPU compartment. This compartment is a different size and the side cleat is on the right. The drawer compartment is also mounted flush with the front face of the return leg.

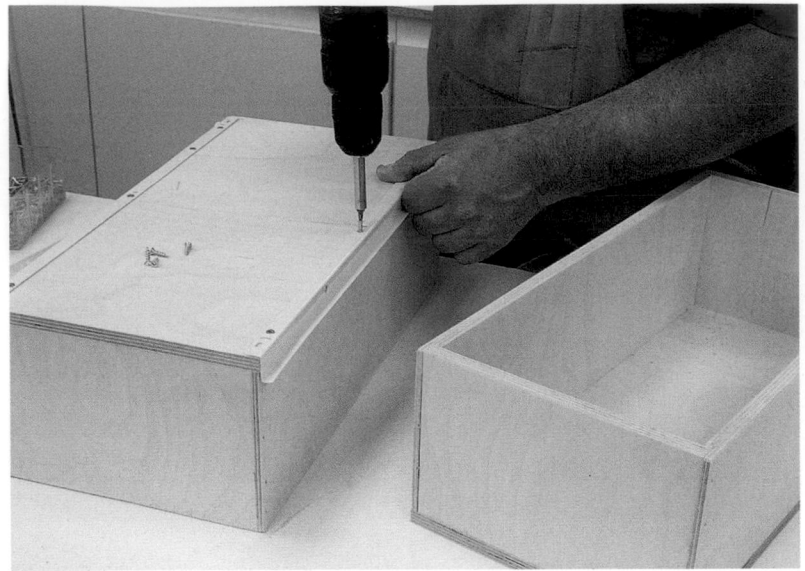

[22] The drawers are made with ½"-thick Baltic birch plywood. Cut all the parts to size as detailed in the cutting list. Assemble the drawers following the procedures outlined in chapter three. This compartment will hold two 6"-high drawers and one top drawer that is 5" high. Space the 18"-long bottom-mount drawer glides 7" apart beginning at the bottom.

[23] The drawer faces are made to match the CPU door. Begin with three pieces of ¾"-thick veneer plywood 5 ⅞" high by 10" wide. Attach ½"-high by ¾"-thick strips on all door edges. Fill the nail holes, sand and round over the front face edges. Install the drawer faces on the boxes with two 1"-long screws through the inside into the drawer face back. Start installing the faces from the bottom; make sure the bottom face is flush with the lower edge of the bottom board. Space the drawer faces ⅛6" apart.

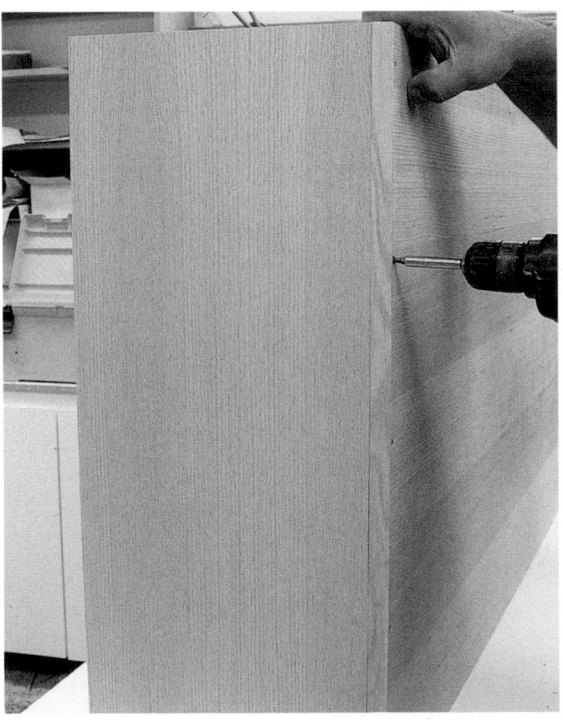

[24] The backboards for the hutch's two side edges, which are 28" high, require wood veneer edge tape. The side boards need a 28"-high edge on each covered with veneer. These will be the front edges. Attach the hutch backboard to the side boards with glue and 2" screws. My hutch will be against a wall so the screw heads do not need to be covered.

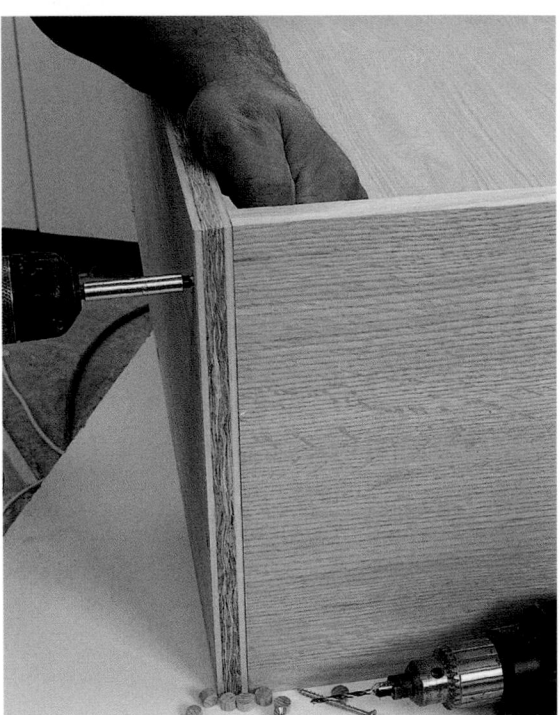

[25] Use glue and 2" screws in counterbored holes to secure the top board (MM) to the sides and back. Fill the holes with wood plugs. The board edges do not have to be covered because a moulding strip will hide them.

[26] Install a moulding strip on the front and two side top edges. Choose any moulding that's suitable as long as it's at least ¾" high. Miter the corners at 45° and secure the strip with glue and finishing nails.

[27] The divider and compartment section is built as a unit and installed in the hutch. If you wish to use the same design as shown here, cut all the parts to size as detailed in the cutting list. Apply wood veneer edge tape to all exposed edges before joining the boards. The section is assembled using simple butt joints with glue and 2" screws. Remember to counterbore any screw head that will be visible so it can be hidden with a wood plug.

Construction Notes

I finished my project with three coats of oil-based polyurethane. After the final coat I applied clear paste wax with extra-fine steel wool. That process made the top smooth and added a little extra protection to the working surface.

The desk and return are designed to accept "compartments" for drawers, cabinets with shelves, or other specialized spaces. If you need a file drawer, build the compartment to meet your size requirements. The CPU section can be fitted with adjustable shelves. The design is versatile and can be altered to meet almost anyone's needs.

The compartment and divider section is another module that can easily be altered to solve your storage problems. Add or remove dividers to accommodate books, software or other documents that must be retrieved many times a day.

I used ¾"-thick veneer plywood. It is an expensive sheet material. But the plywood core is strong and I feel it's well worth the added cost. This work center will be under heavy use and should be built to provide many years of service.

Oak veneer plywood was my choice but there are many other veneer plywoods on the market. If you want to lower the cost, try using MDF for the panels and poplar for the legs. They are perfect materials to paint.

Everyone has different requirements to make the workday easier. This project was designed so it could be customized to meet those specialized needs.

[28] Put the divider section into the hutch and secure with 1"-long screws through the top and sides. Counterbore the holes and fill with a wood plug.

credenza & Bookcase Hutch

Here is a project that will go a long way toward meeting our home office storage requirements. This credenza and bookcase hutch project is an ideal place to store all your stationery and reference materials. Everything is stored in one place so it's a breeze to quickly get what you need. The door cabinets and drawer assembly can be modified to meet your specific needs. Or, leave that section out and the credenza can be used as a desk or worktable because it's 30" high.

Once again I've used one of my favorite building materials — multi-core veneer-covered plywood. It's strong, stable, and can be glued, screwed or nailed. Threaded fasteners work great in this material as long as the proper pilot hole is drilled. Plate joinery, commonly called biscuit joints, is another option that I often use with great success when building furniture with this material.

The credenza top and cabinet legs are solid wood. I've opted for red oak once again but any wood species that matches your décor is perfectly acceptable.

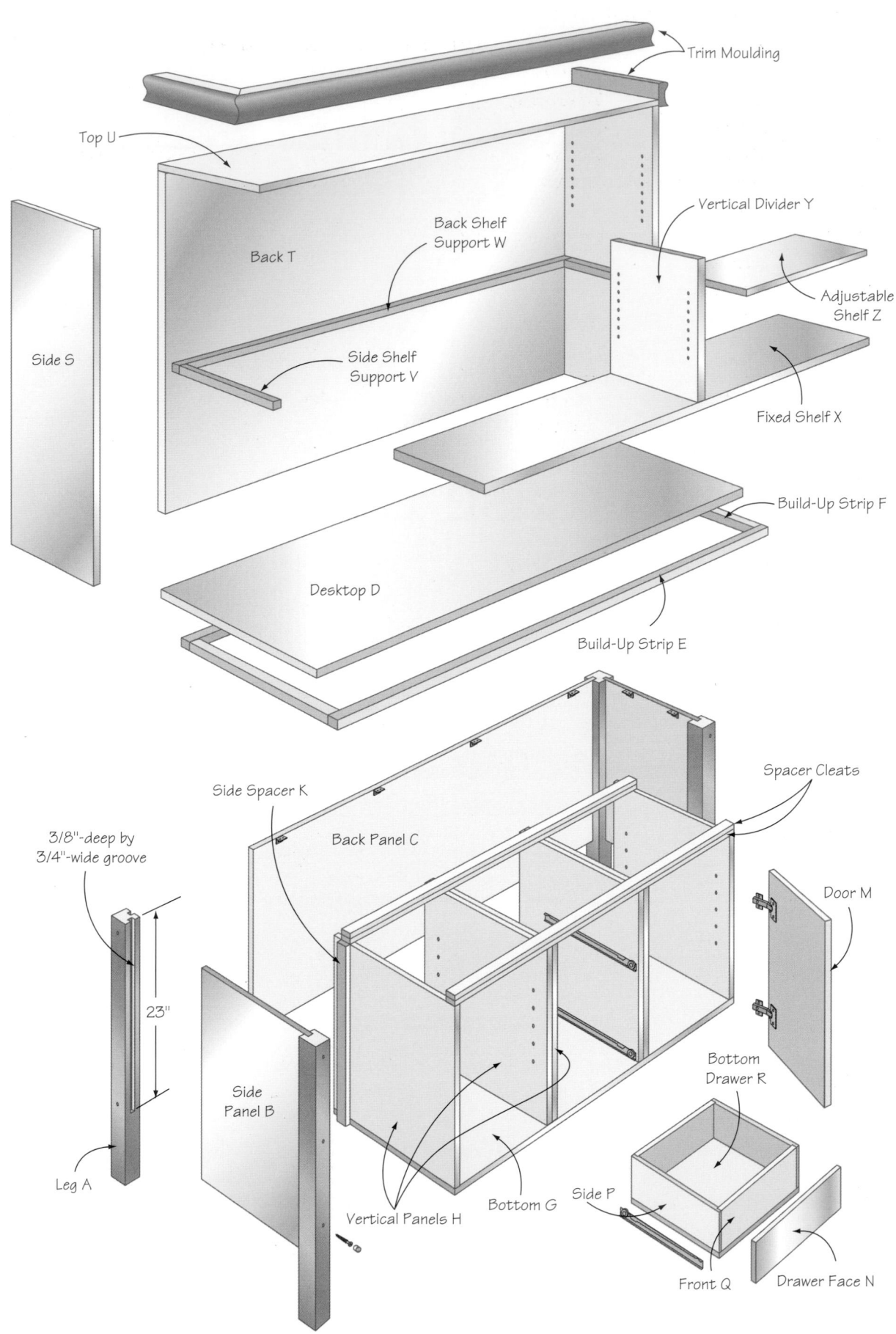

Trim Moulding

Top U

Back T

Back Shelf
Support W

Vertical Divider Y

Adjustable
Shelf Z

Side S

Side Shelf
Support V

Fixed Shelf X

Build-Up Strip F

Desktop D

Build-Up Strip E

Spacer Cleats

Side Spacer K

Back Panel C

3/8"-deep by
3/4"-wide groove

Door M

23"

Side
Panel B

Bottom
Drawer R

Leg A

Vertical Panels H

Bottom G

Side P

Front Q

Drawer Face N

Cutting List • Credenza & Bookcase Hutch

REF.	QTY.	PART	MATERIAL	THICKNESS	WIDTH	LENGTH	COMMENTS
A	4	Legs	Solid oak	1⅝	1⅝	29¼	
B	2	Side panels	Oak veneer ply	¾	23	17	
C	1	Back panel	Oak veneer ply	¾	23	56	
D	1	Desktop	Solid oak	¾	21½	60½	Make from glued-up boards
E	2	Back/front build-up strip	Solid oak	¾	¾	60½	
F	2	Side build-up strips	Solid oak	¾	¾	20	
G	1	Bottom	Oak veneer ply	¾	18¼	55¼	
H	6	Vertical panels	Oak veneer ply	¾	18¼	20¾	
J	4	Spacer cleats	Oak veneer ply	¾	1½	55¼	
K	2	Side spacers	Oak veneer ply	7/16	1½	20¾	
L	2	Shelves	Oak veneer ply	¾	15⅞	18	
M	2	Doors	Oak veneer ply	¾	17	21⅞	
N	2	Drawer faces	Oak veneer ply	¾	10⅞	19¾	
P	4	Drawer sides	Baltic birch ply	½	8⅞	18	
Q	4	Drawer fronts/backs	Baltic birch ply	½	8⅞	17¼	
R	2	Drawer bottoms	Baltic birch ply	½	17¾	18	
Bookcase Hutch							
S	2	Sides	Oak veneer ply	¾	11¼	47¾	
T	1	Back	Oak veneer ply	¾	47¾	60	
U	1	Top	Oak veneer ply	¾	12	60	
V	2	Side shelf supports	Solid wood	¾	1½	11	
W	1	Back shelf support	Oak veneer ply	¾	1½	58½	
X	1	Fixed bottom shelf	Oak veneer ply	¾	11¼	58½	
Y	1	Vertical divider	Oak veneer ply	¾	11¼	27¼	
Z	2	Adjustable shelves	Oak veneer ply	¾	11¼	28 13/16	

Hardware and Supplies

- Screws
- Nails
- Glue
- Biscuits or dowels
- Three-quarter extension drawer glides
- Full-extension drawer glides for the file drawer
- 107° hidden hinges
- Drawer and door handles
- Metal brackets
- Adjustable shelf pins

Metric Cutting List • Credenza & Bookcase Hutch

REF.	QTY.	PART	MATERIAL	THICKNESS	WIDTH	LENGTH	COMMENTS
A	4	Legs	Solid oak	41	41	743	
B	2	Side panels	Oak veneer ply	19	584	432	
C	1	Back panel	Oak veneer ply	19	584	1422	
D	1	Desktop	Solid oak	19	546	1537	Make from glued-up boards
E	2	Back/front build-up strip	Solid oak	19	19	1537	
F	2	Side build-up strips	Solid oak	19	19	508	
G	1	Bottom	Oak veneer ply	19	463	1403	
H	6	Vertical panels	Oak veneer ply	19	463	527	
J	4	Spacer cleats	Oak veneer ply	19	38	1403	
K	2	Side spacers	Oak veneer ply	11	38	527	
L	2	Shelves	Oak veneer ply	19	403	457	
M	2	Doors	Oak veneer ply	19	432	555	
N	2	Drawer faces	Oak veneer ply	19	276	502	
P	4	Drawer sides	Baltic birch ply	13	225	457	
Q	4	Drawer fronts/backs	Baltic birch ply	13	225	438	
R	2	Drawer bottoms	Baltic birch ply	13	451	457	

Bookcase Hutch

REF.	QTY.	PART	MATERIAL	THICKNESS	WIDTH	LENGTH	COMMENTS
S	2	Sides	Oak veneer ply	19	285	1213	
T	1	Back	Oak veneer ply	19	1213	1524	
U	1	Top	Oak veneer ply	19	305	1524	
V	2	Side shelf supports	Solid wood	19	38	279	
W	1	Back shelf support	Oak veneer ply	19	38	1486	
X	1	Fixed bottom shelf	Oak veneer ply	19	285	1486	
Y	1	Vertical divider	Oak veneer ply	19	285	692	
Z	2	Adjustable shelves	Oak veneer ply	19	285	732	

[1] Prepare the four legs for the storage credenza by cutting them to size. The legs require a groove that's ¾"-wide by ⅜"-deep by 23"-long measured from the top of each leg. Two of the legs need a groove on one face. And the two back legs require two grooves on adjoining faces. Center the grooves on the leg faces. The simplest way to make the grooves is with a ¾"-wide router bit in a table-mounted router.

[2] Replace the straight router bit with a ⅜" roundover bit and ease all the edges on each leg. Now is an ideal time to sand the legs.

[3] The straight router bit will leave a rounded end on each groove. Use a sharp chisel to square the ends so the panels will fit correctly.

[4] Cut the two side and back panels to size. The panel ends fit in the grooves of the legs with the double-grooved legs at the back. Put glue in the joint and drive 2" wood screws through the legs and into the panel ends. Two screws per panel end will secure the joint. Drill a pilot hole for the screws and a counterbored ⅜" hole for the screw head. Fill the holes with wood plugs and sand smooth.

[5] Attach seven right-angle brackets to the top edge of the panels. Two per side and three on the back panel will be used to secure the credenza top.

[6] The finished size for the solid wood top will be 21½"-deep by 60½"-wide. Glue up enough ¾"-thick boards to form a top that's about 1" greater in size (biscuit joints are an ideal way to do this). A jointer will dress the edges perfectly, or you can get acceptable glue edges by cutting the boards on a well-tuned table saw. If you don't have a jointer and your saw can't cut a fine edge, most lumberyards will dress the boards for a small fee.

TIP

Don't clamp the boards too tightly when edge joining. Excessive pressure will squeeze out all the glue and the joint will fail. And you shouldn't have to force the joints together if properly edge-dressed.

[7] Sand the top smooth and trim to the correct finished size. Attach the build-up strips and secure with glue and brad nails. This will make the top appear thicker and heavier.

[8] Use a small circular object to draw an arc at each corner of the top. Remove the wood outside the arc with a belt sander to round each corner. Next, install a ⅜" roundover bit in your router and dress the bottom and top edges.

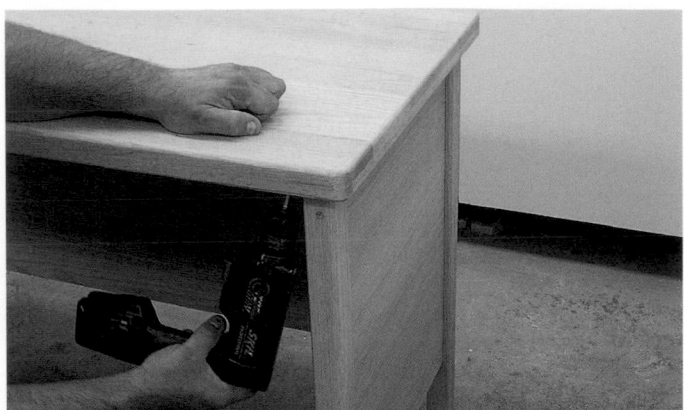

[9] Attach the top to the credenza base with ⅝"-long screws through the right-angle brackets. Verify that the top overhangs all leg faces by 1" before installing the screws. Do not use glue so the top can expand and contract during humidity level changes.

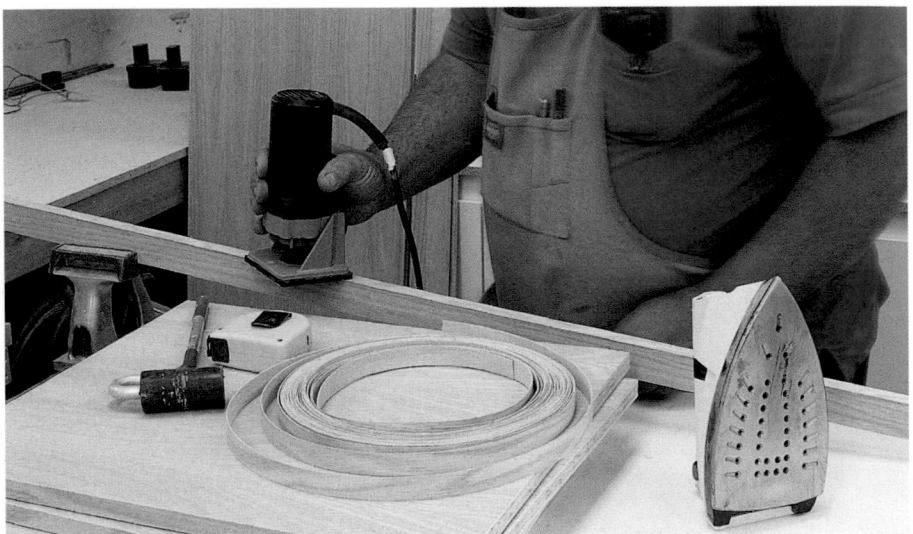

[10] Cut all the panels for the drawer/door compartment. Apply iron-on wood veneer edge tape to the front long edge of the bottom board, the long edge of one spacer cleat, and the long front edge of each vertical panel.

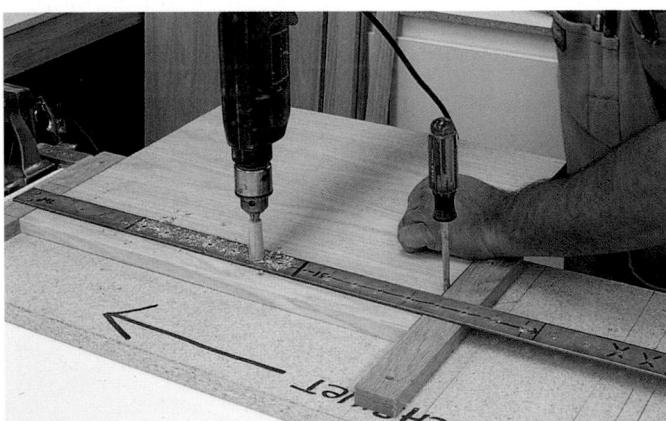

[11] Drill holes in four of the vertical panels for the adjustable shelf pins you plan to use. You can make a simple shelf pin hole jig with flat iron and a couple of pieces of scrap lumber. Drill holes in the iron, spacing them about 1½" apart. Attach the iron to two wood cleats and use a dowel rod mounted on the drill bit to limit the hole depth.

[12] Assemble the credenza with glue and 2" screws according to the illustration. The drawers will be in the center so the four panels with the shelf pin holes will be located facing each other on the two outside compartments. The cleat with the veneered edge is the lower front spacer cleat. Attach the front cleats flush with the front edge of the vertical panels. The rear cleats are spaced 1" in from the ends of all the panels to clear the countertop clips. Verify that the vertical panels are aligned and oriented correctly. The panels must be parallel to each other so the drawer hardware will operate properly.

[13] Glue and nail the 7/16" spacer cleats on the rear outside faces of each end panel, 1" in from the back edge.

[14] Lay the credenza on its back and install the compartment. Use 2" screws through the front panels into the front legs. Use 1½" screws through the rear end of each outside panel, through the side spacers, and into the inside face of each end panel. Drive an additional four 2" screws through the outside face of the rear credenza panel into the back edge of the bottom compartment board. Cut and apply edge tape to one front edge of both adjustable shelf boards.

[16] Cut all the drawer parts to size. Remember to rabbet the back and front ends of each side ¼" deep by ½" wide. Once again, I've used ½"-thick Baltic birch plywood as I feel it's one of the best choices for office furniture drawer boxes. Follow the assembly procedures in chapter four. The finished size of each drawer is 9⅜"-high by 18¾"-wide by 18"-deep. Install the bottom-mounted drawer glide and test fit both boxes. The first box is mounted ⅛" above the bottom board, and there should be a 1" space between the bottom and top box.

[15] The finished size for each door is 17"-wide by 21⅞"-high. You'll need two ¾"-thick wood veneer plywood panels 16"-wide by 20⅞"-high and about 15' of ½"-high by ¾"-thick solid wood to edge the panels. Build the two doors following the same procedures as detailed in chapter six. Round over the front face edges with a ⅜" router bit, drill the hinge holes and install the doors following the steps in chapter five.

[17] Two drawer faces, ¾"-thick by 10⅞"-high by 19¾"-wide, are required. They are built to match the door style with a blank ¾" veneer panel that's 9⅞" high by 18¾" wide. The panel is edged with ½"-high by ¾"-thick solid wood. Secure the drawer faces to the drawer boxes using four 1"-long screws from inside the drawer. The height of both drawer faces, plus a ⅛" space between them, should equal the door height.

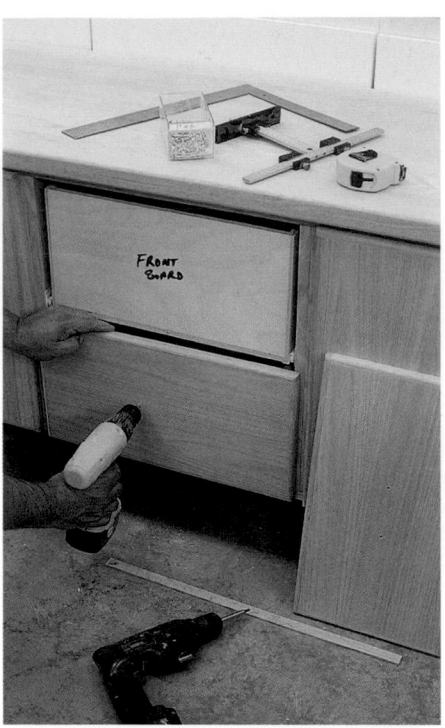

[18] The two side and vertical panels for the bookcase hutch require adjustable shelf pin holes. Begin drilling the holes starting 3" from the top edge of each board to a measurement 24" below the top edges. Space the holes 1¼" apart. The side panels each have two rows of holes on the inside face while the vertical divider (Y) requires holes on both faces. Drill the holes all the way through the divider panel. Apply wood edge veneer tape to one long edge on each board.

[19] Prepare the backboard by applying wood veneer tape to two short edges. These edges will be visible on each side of the hutch. Attach the side boards to the backboard with glue and 2"-long screws. The outside faces of the side boards should be flush with the ends of the backboard and the shelf pin holes oriented properly.

[20] Install the top board on the top edges of the side and back boards using glue and 2" screws. The edges of this panel do not require wood veneer tape, as they will be hidden with trim moulding. It isn't necessary to hide the screw heads, as the top will be on the credenza and over 6' in height.

[21] The lower fixed shelf supports are made with 1x2 solid wood. They are cut at 45° to meet in the back corners. Before cutting the miters, round over the bottom edge as well as the front ends on the side supports. Use glue and 1¼" screws to secure the supports. The screws on the outside face of each side panel should be installed in counterbored holes that can be filled with wood plugs. The supports are secured 28" below the underside of the top board.

[22] Dress one long front edge of the bottom fixed shelf with wood edge tape. Put the shelf on the supports; secure with glue and brad nails.

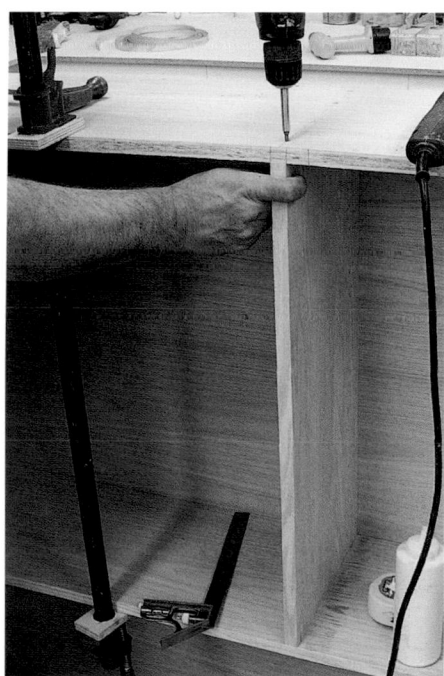

[23] Apply wood edge tape to the front of the vertical divider and secure it in place. Use glue and 2" screws through the top and bottom boards. The holes on the underside of the bottom board should be counterbored and filled with plugs.

[24] Install trim moulding around the top board. I am using the same trim moulding as in chapter six to match the desk hutch. Cut the two adjustable shelves, tape the front edges, and install them on shelf pins.

Construction Notes

The hutch can be secured to the credenza with screws through the underside of the top. One screw at each end, driven into the bottom of the side boards, will hold the hutch securely.

This project was finished with three coats of semi-gloss polyurethane. I used extra-fine steel wool to apply a low-luster paste wax to the finished piece for smoothness and extra protection.

As I mentioned throughout the project, both credenza and hutch can be modified to suit your requirements. If you require a file drawer in the credenza, adjust the compartment dimensions accordingly. These projects offer flexibility, as everyone's office functions differently.

If the cost of veneer plywood is an issue, consider using MDF and a paint finish. If you want high-end furniture, use solid wood panels with more complicated joinery. Either way, you'll save money and get better quality compared to commercial, store-bought furniture, and each piece can be customized to meet your personal requirements.

chapter eight

armoire Work Center

An armoire work center addresses many housekeeping problems for the busy home worker. Most importantly, it organizes all your documents and equipment in one place. You don't have to lug everything out each time you begin working — just open the doors and start being productive. When you have guests drop in, simply close the doors. It's an instant office that's perfect for the bedroom, family room or a large kitchen. And though it's not very difficult to build, this project is one that will be greatly appreciated by any busy home-office worker.

This armoire has large doors with bulletin and memo boards on the back side. There's even a place to hold documents that you need to access quickly and easily. The adjustable bookshelf is large enough to store CDs, books and directories, and the drawer bank has two utility drawers, as well as a hanging file drawer. The computer monitor sits directly above a large keyboard tray, and the computer CPU can be mounted on a pull-out tray for easier disk insertion and removal. There's even a place available for storing all of your paper supplies.

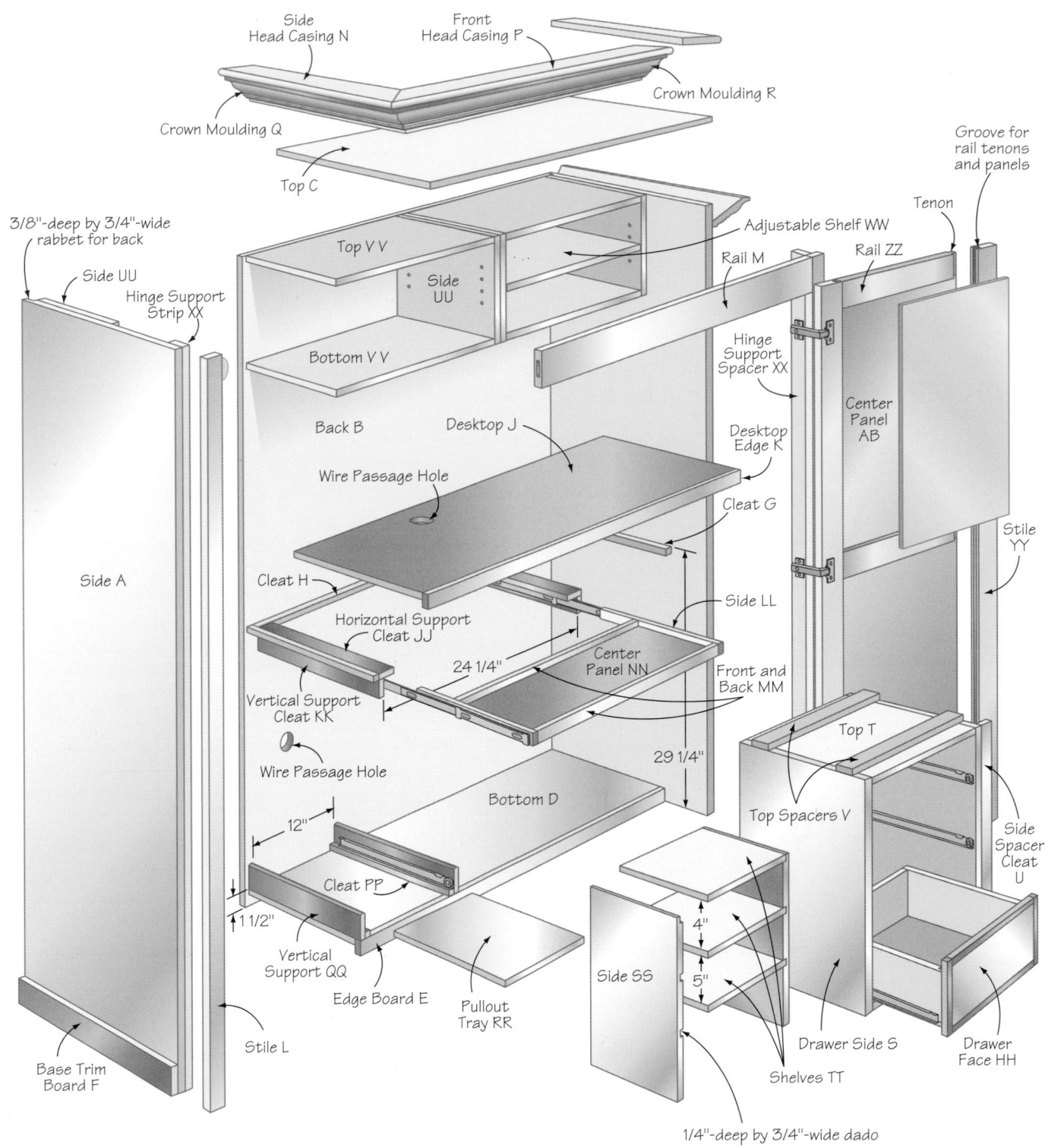

Side Head Casing N

Front Head Casing P

Crown Moulding R

Crown Moulding Q

Top C

3/8"-deep by 3/4"-wide rabbet for back

Side UU

Hinge Support Strip XX

Top V V

Side UU

Adjustable Shelf WW

Rail M

Hinge Support Spacer XX

Rail ZZ

Groove for rail tenons and panels

Tenon

Bottom V V

Back B

Desktop J

Wire Passage Hole

Desktop Edge K

Center Panel AB

Cleat G

Side A

Cleat H

Side LL

Horizontal Support Cleat JJ

24 1/4"

Center Panel NN

Front and Back MM

Stile YY

Vertical Support Cleat KK

Wire Passage Hole

29 1/4"

Top T

Top Spacers V

Side Spacer Cleat U

Bottom D

12"

Cleat PP

1 1/2"

Vertical Support QQ

Edge Board E

Pullout Tray RR

Side SS

4"

5"

Drawer Side S

Drawer Face HH

Base Trim Board F

Stile L

Shelves TT

1/4"-deep by 3/4"-wide dado

Cutting List • Armoire Work Center

REF.	QTY.	PART	MATERIAL	THICKNESS	WIDTH	LENGTH	COMMENTS
A	2	Sides	Oak veneer ply	¾	23¼	72	
B	1	Back	Oak veneer ply	¾	48	72	
C	1	Top	Oak veneer ply	¾	22½	47¼	
D	1	Bottom	Oak veneer ply	¾	15¼	47¼	
E	1	Bottom edge board	Solid oak	¾	1½	47¼	
F	2	Base trim boards	Solid oak	¾	3½	23¼	
G	2	Desktop cleats	Solid oak	¾	¾	18¾	
H	1	Desktop cleat	Solid oak	¾	¾	45¾	
J	1	Desktop	Oak veneer ply	¾	18¾	47¼	
K	1	Desktop edge	Solid oak	¾	1½	47¼	
L	2	Stiles	Solid oak	¾	1½	72	
M	1	Rail	Solid oak	¾	5¼	45¾	
N	2	Side head casing	Solid oak	¾	3¼	26⅞	Angle cut
P	1	Front head casing	Solid oak	¾	3¼	54¾	Angle cut
Q	2	Side crown moulding	Solid oak	¾	3⅛	26¼	Angle cut
R	1	Front crown moulding	Solid oak	¾	3⅛	53¼	Angle cut

Drawer Compartment & Drawers

REF.	QTY.	PART	MATERIAL	THICKNESS	WIDTH	LENGTH	COMMENTS
S	2	Sides	Oak veneer ply	¾	18¾	27	
T	1	Bottom and top	Oak veneer ply	¾	18¾	17¼	
U	1	Side spacer cleat	Oak veneer ply	¾	2	27	
V	2	Top spacers	Oak veneer ply	¾	2	18	
W	2	Top drawer sides	Baltic birch ply	½	4½	18	
X	2	Drawer front & back	Baltic birch ply	½	4½	15¾	
Y	1	Top drawer bottom	Baltic birch ply	½	16¼	18	
Z	2	Middle drawer sides	Baltic birch ply	½	5	18	
AA	2	Front and back	Baltic birch ply	½	5	15¾	
BB	1	Middle drawer bottom	Baltic birch ply	½	16¼	18	
CC	2	File drawer sides	Baltic birch ply	½	10	18	
DD	2	Front and back	Baltic birch ply	½	10	15¾	
EE	1	File drawer bottom	Baltic birch ply	½	16¼	18	
FF	1	Top drawer face	Oak veneer ply	¾	6½	18½	Edge with wood veneer tape
GG	1	Middle drawer face	Oak veneer ply	¾	6½	18½	Edge with wood veneer tape
HH	1	Bottom drawer face	Oak veneer ply	¾	13½	18½	Edge with wood veneer tape

Keyboard Pull-Out

REF.	QTY.	PART	MATERIAL	THICKNESS	WIDTH	LENGTH	COMMENTS
JJ	2	Horizontal support cleats	Oak veneer ply	¾	3¼	18	
KK	2	Vertical support cleats	Solid oak	¾	3¼	18	
LL	2	Sides	Solid oak	¾	1½	18	
MM	2	Front and back	Oak veneer ply	¾	1½	21¾	
NN	1	Center panel	Oak veneer ply	¾	21¾	12½	

Cutting List (continued) • Armoire Work Center

REF.	QTY.	PART	MATERIAL	THICKNESS	WIDTH	LENGTH	COMMENTS
CPU Pull-Out							
PP	2	Cleats	Solid oak	¾	¾	16	
QQ	2	Vertical supports	Solid oak	¾	3½	16	
RR	1	Pull-out tray	Solid oak	¾	11	16	
Paper Storage Shelf							
SS	2	Sides	Oak veneer ply	¾	11	20	
TT	3	Shelves	Oak veneer ply	¾	11	12	
Bookcase							
UU	4	Sides	Oak veneer ply	¾	12	20	
VV	4	Bottoms and tops	Oak veneer ply	¾	12	22⅛	
WW	2	Adjustable shelves	Oak veneer ply	¾	12	22	
Doors							
XX	2	Hinge support spacers	Oak veneer ply	¾	3	71¼	
YY	4	Stiles	Solid oak	¾	3	67	
ZZ	6	Rails	Solid oak	¾	3	18⅜	
AB	4	Center panels	Oak veneer ply	¼	18¼	30	

Hardware and Supplies

Screws

Nails

Glue

Biscuits or dowels

Three-quarter extension drawer glides

Full-extension drawer glides for the file drawer

107° hidden hinges

170° hidden hinges

Cable hole grommets

Commercial CD racks (optional)

Pull-out keyboard tray

Drawer and door handles

Metal brackets

Metric Cutting List • Armoire Work Center

REF.	QTY.	PART	MATERIAL	THICKNESS	WIDTH	LENGTH	COMMENTS
A	2	Sides	Oak veneer ply	19	590	1829	
B	1	Back	Oak veneer ply	19	1219	1829	
C	1	Top	Oak veneer ply	19	572	1200	
D	1	Bottom	Oak veneer ply	19	387	1200	
E	1	Bottom edge board	Solid oak	19	38	1200	
F	2	Base trim boards	Solid oak	19	89	590	
G	2	Desktop cleats	Solid oak	19	19	476	
H	1	Desktop cleat	Solid oak	19	19	1162	
J	1	Desktop	Oak veneer ply	19	476	1200	
K	1	Desktop edge	Solid oak	19	38	1200	
L	2	Stiles	Solid oak	19	38	1829	
M	1	Rail	Solid oak	19	133	1162	
N	2	Side head casing	Solid oak	19	82	682	Angle cut
P	1	Front head casing	Solid oak	19	82	1391	Angle cut
Q	2	Side crown moulding	Solid oak	19	79	666	Angle cut
R	1	Front crown moulding	Solid oak	19	79	1352	Angle cut

Drawer Compartment & Drawers

REF.	QTY.	PART	MATERIAL	THICKNESS	WIDTH	LENGTH	COMMENTS
S	2	Sides	Oak veneer ply	19	476	686	
T	1	Bottom and top	Oak veneer ply	19	476	438	
U	1	Side spacer cleat	Oak veneer ply	19	51	686	
V	2	Top spacers	Oak veneer ply	19	51	457	
W	2	Top drawer sides	Baltic birch ply	13	115	457	
X	2	Drawer front & back	Baltic birch ply	13	115	400	
Y	1	Top drawer bottom	Baltic birch ply	13	412	457	
Z	2	Middle drawer sides	Baltic birch ply	13	127	457	
AA	2	Front and back	Baltic birch ply	13	127	400	
BB	1	Middle drawer bottom	Baltic birch ply	13	412	457	
CC	2	File drawer sides	Baltic birch ply	13	254	457	
DD	2	Front and back	Baltic birch ply	13	254	400	
EE	1	File drawer bottom	Baltic birch ply	13	412	457	
FF	1	Top drawer face	Oak veneer ply	19	165	470	Edge with wood veneer tape
GG	1	Middle drawer face	Oak veneer ply	19	165	470	Edge with wood veneer tape
HH	1	Bottom drawer face	Oak veneer ply	19	343	470	Edge with wood veneer tape

Keyboard Pull-Out

REF.	QTY.	PART	MATERIAL	THICKNESS	WIDTH	LENGTH	COMMENTS
JJ	2	Horizontal support cleats	Oak veneer ply	19	82	457	
KK	2	Vertical support cleats	Solid oak	19	82	457	
LL	2	Sides	Solid oak	19	38	457	
MM	2	Front and back	Oak veneer ply	19	38	552	
NN	1	Center panel	Oak veneer ply	19	552	318	

Metric Cutting List (continued) • Armoire Work Center

REF.	QTY.	PART	MATERIAL	THICKNESS	WIDTH	LENGTH	COMMENTS
CPU Pull-Out							
PP	2	Cleats	Solid oak	19	19	406	
QQ	2	Vertical supports	Solid oak	19	89	406	
RR	1	Pull-out tray	Solid oak	19	279	406	
Paper Storage Shelf							
SS	2	Sides	Oak veneer ply	19	279	508	
TT	3	Shelves	Oak veneer ply	19	279	305	
Bookcase							
UU	4	Sides	Oak veneer ply	19	305	508	
VV	4	Bottoms and tops	Oak veneer ply	19	305	562	
WW	2	Adjustable shelves	Oak veneer ply	19	305	559	
Doors							
XX	2	Hinge support spacers	Oak veneer ply	19	76	1809	
YY	4	Stiles	Solid oak	19	76	1702	
ZZ	6	Rails	Solid oak	19	76	467	
AB	4	Center panels	Oak veneer ply	6	463	762	

[1] Prepare both side panels by cutting a ¾"-wide by ⅜"-deep rabbet on the inside back edge of each panel. Use a router and straight bit with a guide, or form the rabbet on a router table.

[2] The backboard is secured to the two side panels in the rabbet cuts. Use glue and 2" finishing nails driven from the backside of the panel into the side edges.

[3] The top board is attached to the sides and backboard with glue and 2" screws. It's installed flush with the top edges of both sides as well as the backboard. The screws can be driven through the side panels because the heads will be covered with trim molding.

[4] Cut the bottom board to size as detailed in the cutting list. You'll also need to prepare the solid wood strip (E) to cover the front edge on this panel. The edge strip should be rounded over on the front face with a ⅜" roundover bit. Attach it to the bottom board, with its top edge flush with the top surface of the panel, using glue and biscuits or nails. Install the bottom board using glue and 2"-long screws driven through the sides and back panel. The top surface of this board should be 1½" above the bottom edges of the sides and back panels.

[5] The solid wood base trim boards (F) are installed on the lower end of each side panel. Before securing the boards, use a ⅜" roundover bit to remove the top and both end edges. Attach the trim pieces with glue and 1¼" screws. The screw heads are installed under the bottom board, and the trim is clamped only where the screw heads would be visible in front of the bottom board.

TIP

Predrill the holes in each cleat for screws that will be used to support the desktop. The cleats are only ¾" wide and it's difficult to get a drill located correctly after they are installed. Use a bit larger than the screw shaft so the desktop will be tightly drawn to the cleat surface. The screws can only spin freely in the cleats and thread tightly in the underside of the desktop, securing it properly.

[6] Secure the three desktop support cleats (G and H) with glue and 1¼" screws. Predrill the holes in the cleats to avoid cracking the thin strips. Attach the cleats so their top edges are 29¼" above the floor.

[7] The desktop (J) requires a hardwood edge strip (K), similar to the bottom board. Dress the hardwood edge with a ⅜" router bit after attaching it to the desktop. Secure the completed top to the support cleats with glue and 1¼" screws.

[8] Cut the two stiles (L) and install one before proceeding further. The stiles are secured flush with the outside face of each side panel and secured with glue and finishing nails. Countersink the nail holes and fill with wood putty.

[9] The upper rail (M) is secured with glue and biscuits into the stile edges. It is also face nailed to the edge of the top board. If you don't own a biscuit joiner, use dowels or small wood blocks on the backside to attach the rail and stiles. Install the second stile now.

[10] While the cabinet is on its back, cut and install the head casing. The trim is made by rounding over the front edge of a 1x4 board and cutting it to size. Once the edge is rounded over, cut the 45° mitered corners. This head casing extends 2½" past the front and side faces of the cabinet. It's secured with glue and 1¼" screws.

TIP

Now is a great time to sand the face frame smooth. It's also worth taking time to fill the nail head holes before the crown moulding is attached.

[Cutting Crown Moulding]

Crown moulding can be accurately cut at 45° if placed correctly in your miter box or saw. Always place the crown upside-down on the miter saw. In other words, think of the saw table as the ceiling and the backboard as the wall surface. Orient the crown so its top rests squarely on the saw table and the bottom tightly against the saw backstop. You'll get a perfect miter cut each and every time.

[11] Stock 3⅛"-high crown moulding is glued and nailed at an angle between the cabinet and head casing. You'll need three pieces cut at a 45° angle as detailed in the cutting list.

[12] Use a ⅜" roundover bit in a handheld router to ease the outside edges of both cabinet stiles. The router will stop at the crown, which will be the endpoint of each cut.

[13] The drawer compartment contains two utility drawers and a file drawer. Hanging hardware for file folders requires the supports at 15¼" wide. This dimension determines the width of the drawer compartment. The outside dimensions, using ¾"-thick veneer plywood, will be 18¾"-deep by 18¾"-wide by 27"-high. So with that in mind, cut pieces S and T to size and apply wood veneer edge tape to the outside edges. Join the sides to the bottom and top boards using 2" screws and glue. Counterbore the screw holes on the left hand side and fill with wood plugs. The other side will not be visible.

[14] Attach the spacer cleat (U) to the right front edge of the compartment using glue and screws. This spacer will provide clearance when opening the drawers. A piece of ¾"-thick plywood veneer will work fine. Secure the two top spacers (V) on the underside of the desktop using 1¼" screws. These spacers will fill the compartment-to-desktop gap. Install the compartment and anchor it with two 1¼" screws through the top and bottom boards.

[15] Cut all the pieces of ½"-thick Baltic birch plywood for the three drawer boxes. Each drawer side requires a ½"-wide by ¼"-deep rabbet on both inside ends (refer to the assembly instructions in chapter three when building the drawers). Then install the bottom-mount drawer glides so there's a 2" space above the file drawer and a 1" space above each utility drawer box. Use 18"-long full-extension drawer glides for the file drawer and 18" bottom-mounted glides for the utility drawers. (I've installed 1½"-wide by ⅛"-thick flat aluminum, ⅜" above the drawer edge, to support the hanging file folders — see chapter ten for more details.)

[16] The three drawer faces are made with ¾"-thick veneer plywood. All the edges have iron-on veneer tape to hide the plywood core. The bottom drawer face is installed first and secured flush with the lower edge of the compartment's bottom board. Install the middle face with a 1⁄16" space between faces. The simplest way to locate drawer faces is to drill the handle hole and drive a screw through that hole into the box. This will secure the face until two 1" screws can be installed through the back of the drawer box front board and into the drawer face.

[17] Attach the plywood supports for the keyboard tray to the underside of the desktop with 1¼" screws. Glue and screw the plywood pieces to the solid wood verticals forming two right-angle brackets. Round over the front lower corner on the solid wood supports with a belt sander. Secure the brackets to the desktop so the inside faces of the vertical supports are 24¼" apart.

[18] Assemble the keyboard tray as shown. The hardwood side pieces and the front and back strips are secured with glue and screws so they are ¾" above the plywood veneer panel. Counterbore the screw holes and fill with wood plugs. Use a ¼" roundover bit in a router to ease all the hardwood support edges. The tray is fitted with a 18" full-extension drawer glide. The side pieces are 18" long, but the tray platform, including the hardwood front and back rails, is 14" deep. This will provide room at the back of the pull-out for wires from the keyboard, monitor and printer. Mount the drawer glide cabinet members as low as possible on the support brackets.

[19] Drill a wire passage hole for a grommet at the back of the desktop. Position the hole near the center of the keyboard pull-out tray. Use a large-diameter grommet to accommodate the large printer cable end. Drill an additional hole under the desktop, through the backboard, for a power supply cord.

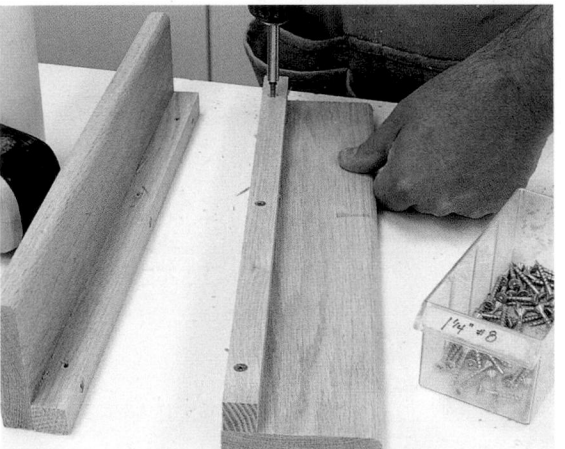

[20] The CPU pull-out is mounted on 16" bottom-mounted drawer glides. Cut the parts and make the two support brackets as shown. Round over the tops of each upright.

[21] Install the CPU pull-out brackets with 1¼" screws driven into the bottom board. Space the inside faces of the vertical members 12" apart. The platform is ¾" veneer plywood with iron-on taped edges. Mount the platform on standard 16" bottom-mounted drawer glides.

[22] Build a paper storage compartment using ¾" veneer plywood and apply wood veneer to the front edges. Dado and rabbet the compartment sides and clamp the assembly until the adhesive sets. Edge tape the boards before making the router cuts so the edge veneer will be cut cleanly. This compartment fits between the CPU pull-out and drawer compartment, and does not have to be secured to the armoire carcass.

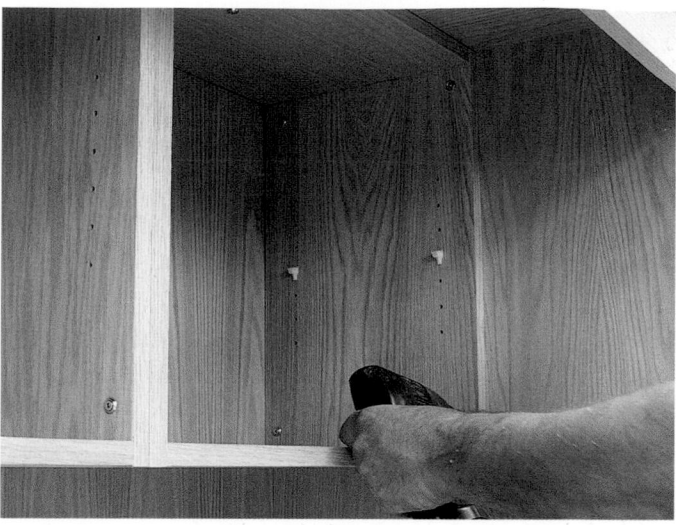

[23] The upper bookcases are two simple boxes with shelf pin holes drilled for adjustable shelving. You must build two boxes, as one full width case cannot be installed in the armoire carcass. Apply wood veneer edge tape to all exposed edges. Join the sides to the bottom and top boards using glue and 2" screws. I installed the cases with 1½"-long screws and decorative washers. I did not glue them in place in case they need to be altered when I purchase new computer equipment.

[Determining Door Size]

The required door width is calculated by adding 1" to the interior cabinet dimension. Inside stile face to inside stile face is 45¾" making the combined door width number 46¾". Dividing this value by two (for two doors) means that each door will be 23⅜" wide. The height is not as critical, but I want the door 1½" off the ground and overlapping part of the top rail. For this application my door height will be 67".

[24] Before constructing the doors, install two hinge plate support spacers as shown here, using 1¼" No. 6 wood screws. These are necessary when using hidden hinges with a standard mounting plate. The cabinet side, where the plates will be attached, must be flush with the inside faces of the stiles. Apply wood veneer edge tape to one long edge of each board. This will be the inside visible edge. Use glue and clamp the supports in place until the adhesive sets.

[25] The four stiles require a groove in the center of one edge that's ¼" wide by ½" deep. These cuts are easily made with a properly aligned table saw.

[26] Four of the rails need a ¼"-wide by ½"-deep groove in the center of one long edge. The remaining two, which are the center rails for each door, require the groove on both long edges.

[27] All the rails require a tenon centered on each end. This tenon is ¼" thick by ½" deep. The table saw is the perfect tool when making these tenons. You'll need to make a number of passes on each board but it's a quick and easy task to complete.

[28] Attach the middle rail in the center of two stiles. Use glue on the tenon and pin the joint with a brad nail on the backside of the door. Dry fit the two end rails by clamping them in place temporarily. Use a ⅜" roundover bit in a router to round over the inside frame edges. Be sure the router bit bearing is riding on solid wood below the grooves.

[29] Cut the four ¼"-thick veneer plywood center panels (AB). Slip the panels into their grooves but don't glue them in place. Apply glue to the tenons on each end rail, install them in the grooves making sure they are flush with the stile ends and clamp each assembly. Pin the tenon with a brad nail on the backside of the door.

TIP

I am using "good one side" (GIS) ¼" veneer plywood for my center panels. It's less expensive than "good two side," and I plan to cover the backside with bulletin and white boards. If you don't want the backs covered, use the "good two side" material.

[30] Once the door joints are set, round over the outside profile using a ⅜" roundover bit.

[31] Drill 35mm-diameter holes, ⅛" from the door edge, for the hidden hinges. Each door will use three 170° hinges. The doors can be mounted using the same procedures as in chapter five. However, you must use standard 100° to 120° hinges when using this mounting procedure. Once correctly located, they can be replaced with the 170° hardware. Attach the mounting plates with 1¼" screws when the door is held 1½" above the floor.

[32] The backs of each door can be fitted with various materials in the center panel area. On one door I've installed a ½"-thick cork bulletin board secured with mirror clips for easy removal and replacement. Remember to drill pilot holes for the screws, as you will be installing them near the frame edges.

[33] Another alternative for door backs is ¼"-thick white board. It makes a great note board for those telephone calls and meeting reminders. I found that common storm window clips made of plastic worked well to hold the panel. It is also easily removed when I want to change boards.

[34] There are dozens of inexpensive plastic trays, bins and paper holders that are available at your local office supply store. You can install any number of these to suit your own requirements. I've used plastic file holder trays and attached them to wood strips. It's the perfect place for active files or phone books.

Construction Notes

- The armoire was finished with three coats of polyurethane. I then rubbed on a hard coat of paste wax with extra-fine steel wool, then buffed all the surfaces.
- The interior compartment positions and sizes can be altered to suit your needs. With the exception of the desktop, which should be 30" above the floor, and the interior width of the hanging file drawer, any layout is possible.
- The bookcase as designed will hold reference manuals, a few CDs and software. But it can be built higher, lower or shorter. If you have a great many CDs, a longer section, extended to the desktop with smaller shelf spacing, is a possible option. For those of you with a number of hardware accessories, consider eliminating one part of the bookcase to make room for an equipment shelf stack. The pull-out tray for the keyboard can be widened to accommodate a mouse pad by lowering the drawer compartment. Or the paper storage shelf can be a printer stand with a few modifications. To summarize, don't assume that my design is the only design — there are many possibilities.
- Though I used oak, any sheet material, such as MDF or plywood, is suitable. And the overall "look" of the cabinet can be changed with different mouldings to match any furniture style. For example, a thin top moulding will make the cabinet appear more streamlined and modern.
- Finally, search the office supply stationery stores for some of the great plastic accessories that can be attached to the doors or installed in the cabinet. They are usually inexpensive and really help to organize your workspace.

chapter nine

office Bookcase

There's always a need for extra book storage in the office. Although we depend heavily on computers, we still require those invaluable reference books.

I made this project using oak veneer plywood and solid woods. The shelves are all adjustable, and I've used a little different technique for the supports in place of the usual holes. These metal shelf standards are installed in a groove, are capable of handling heavy loads and are available in a number of finishes. I used white so it would be easier to see in the photographs; however, gold might be more suitable with the natural clear polyurethane that I've applied. The choice is up to you but is often determined by the final color of the bookcase. One note: Purchase your shelf standards before cutting the grooves. There are size variations depending on the manufacturer, and you want to be sure the cut is correct.

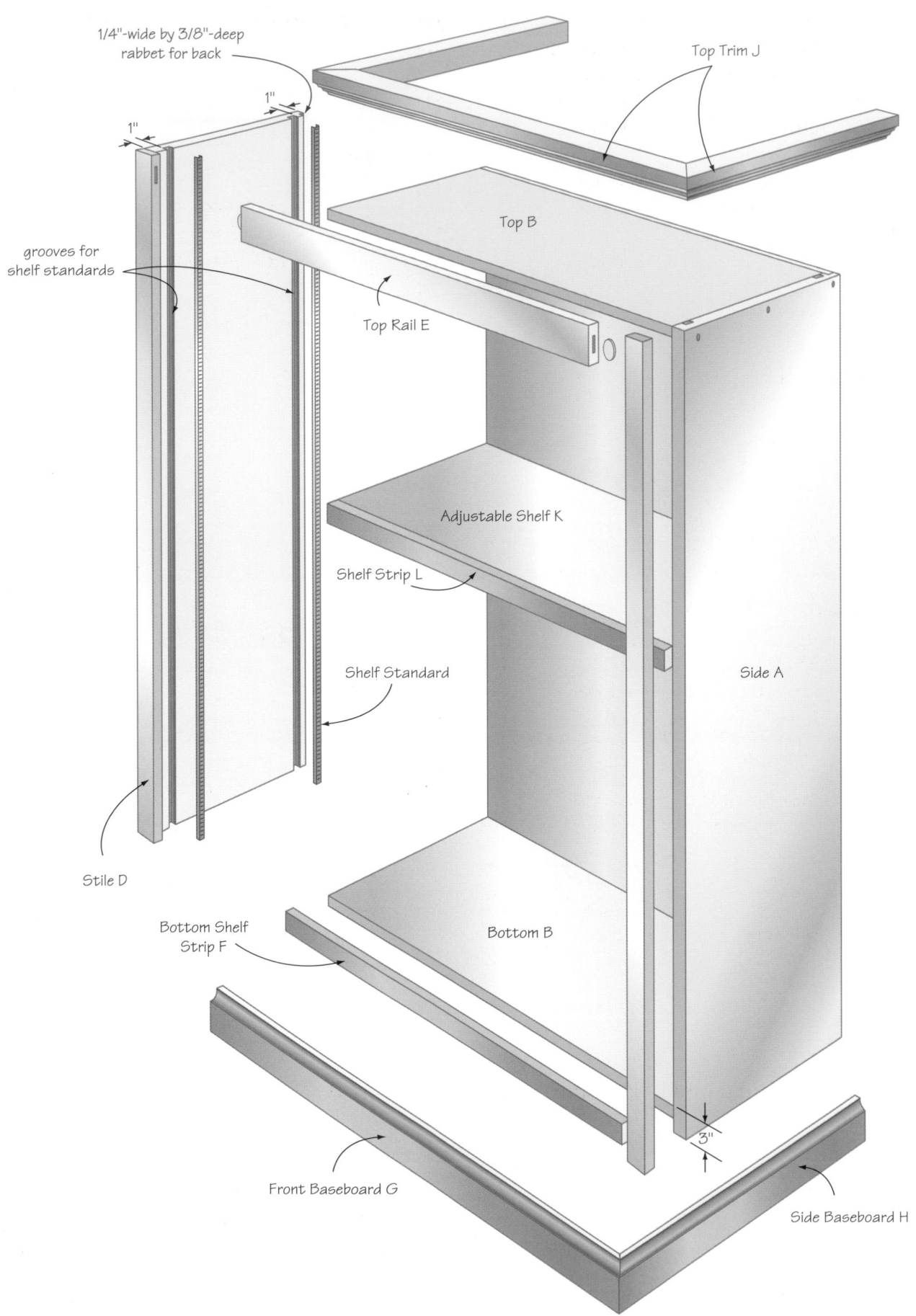

1/4"-wide by 3/8"-deep rabbet for back

1"

1"

Top Trim J

grooves for shelf standards

Top B

Top Rail E

Adjustable Shelf K

Shelf Strip L

Shelf Standard

Side A

Stile D

Bottom Shelf Strip F

Bottom B

Front Baseboard G

3"

Side Baseboard H

Cutting List • Office Bookcase

REF.	QTY.	PART	MATERIAL	THICK	WIDTH	LENGTH	COMMENTS
A	2	Sides	Oak veneer ply	¾	11⅞	78	
B	2	Top and bottom	Oak veneer ply	¾	11⅞	31¾	
C	1	Back	Oak veneer ply	¼	32½	75¾	
D	2	Stiles	Solid wood	¾	1½	78	
E	1	Top rail	Solid wood	¾	3½	30¼	
F	1	Bottom shelf strip	Solid wood	¾	1½	30¼	
G	1	Front baseboard	Solid wood	¾	3	34¾	Angle cut on both ends
H	2	Side baseboards	Solid wood	¾	3	13½	Angle cut on front end
J	7'	Top trim	Solid wood	*	*	*	Depends on style chosen
K	4	Shelves	Oak veneer ply	¾	10⅞	31½	
L	4	Shelf strips	Solid wood	¾	1½	31½	

Hardware and Supplies

Glue

Screws

Shelf standard

Adjustable shelf pins

Biscuits or dowels

Metric Cutting List • Office Bookcase

REF.	QTY.	PART	MATERIAL	THICK	WIDTH	LENGTH	COMMENTS
A	2	Sides	Oak veneer ply	19	301	1981	
B	2	Top and bottom	Oak veneer ply	19	301	806	
C	1	Back	Oak veneer ply	6	826	1924	
D	2	Stiles	Solid wood	19	38	1981	
E	1	Top rail	Solid wood	19	89	768	
F	1	Bottom shelf strip	Solid wood	19	38	768	
G	1	Front baseboard	Solid wood	19	76	883	Angle cut on both ends
H	2	Side baseboards	Solid wood	19	76	343	Angle cut on front end
J	7'	Top trim	Solid wood	*	*	*	Depends on style chosen
K	4	Shelves	Oak veneer ply	19	276	800	
L	4	Shelf strips	Solid wood	19	38	800	

[1] Each side (A) requires a rabbet on the rear inside face that's ⅜" wide by ¼" deep. They also need two grooves 1" in from the edges, for the shelf standards.

[2] The shelf standards should be cut 78" long. Install them in the grooves and use the small nails provided to secure the standards.

[3] Attach the two sides to the top board with glue and 2" screws (it should be flush with the upper ends of the sides). Drive the screws through the outside face on the side panels, as they will be covered with trim. Attach the bottom board in the same way, aligning its top surface 3" above the bottom ends of the sides. The top and bottom boards should be flush with the side boards' front edges.

[4] Use glue and brad nails to attach the backboard. Take a little extra time to cut the back accurately because a squarely cut back will properly align the bookcase carcass.

[5] Attach the stiles flush with the outside face of each side board. There are a number of methods you can use to attach the stiles. Glue and clamps, glue with biscuits, or simply glue and face nailing with finishing nails are all acceptable. I used the glue-and-face-nail method and filled the nail holes with colored wood filler to match my final finish. Install one stile at this time. Attach the other side after the upper rail is secured.

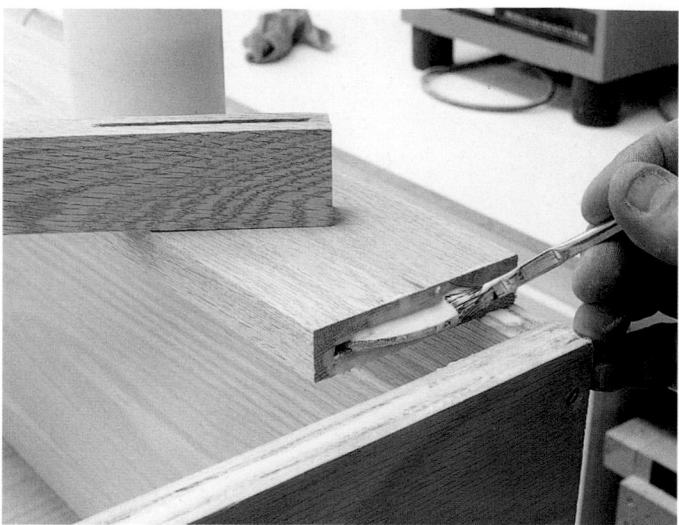

[6] The upper rail is installed with biscuits into the side of each stile. Additionally, apply glue to the edge of the carcass top board and face nail the rail. After the rail is secured, install the remaining stile.

[Adding Some Interest]

You can add a little interest and change the appearance of your bookcase by cutting flutes in the stile faces. A V-bit installed in a router can create an interesting pattern. The cut depth controls flute width.

[7] Attach the hardwood strip (F) to the front edge of the bottom shelf. This will extend the bottom shelf making it flush with the stile faces. Glue and nail the strip in place and don't be concerned about filling the nail head holes as they will be covered by the base trim.

[8] The base trim measurements in the cutting list are taken at the longest point of the 45° angle cuts. The top edge of the trim is decorated with a cove bit in a router. Attach the baseboards with glue and 1¼" screws on the backside. These trim boards should be installed flush with the top surface of the bottom board.

[9] Before installing the top trim, round over the inside edges of the two stiles and top rail with a ⅜" roundover bit. The router base plate will be stopped by the base trim and determines the point at which the roundover stops on each stile.

[Working with Mouldings]

The top moulding can be purchased or made with a router bit. There are dozens of possible patterns. If you make a lot of trim moulding for your projects, a moulding head cutter for the table saw, such as the Magic Molder from LRH Enterprises Inc., is a worthwhile investment.

TIP

You'll get "cleaner"-looking corners on trim boards, with decorative router cuts, by routering the design patterns before mitering the corners. This technique prevents routering mistakes when trying to cut a pattern near a mitered end.

[10] Cut the three pieces of top trim moulding at 45°. Use the dimensions in the cutting list as a guide — verify the measurements on your bookcase before cutting the trim to size. Use glue and nails to attach the moulding.

[12] Cut the four shelf boards (K). The front trim pieces (L) for the shelves will make them appear thicker and add a great deal of strength to the boards. Use glue and nails or biscuits to attach the edges. Round over the top and bottom with a ⅜" roundover bit.

[11] Before standing the bookcase upright, round over the outside edges of both stiles. Use a ⅜" roundover bit in a router. The upper and lower trim boards will stop the router travel and determine the cut length.

Construction Notes

I've finished my bookcase with three coats of semi-gloss polyurethane. The first coat was cut with 10 percent mineral spirits and sanded with 320-grit papers. The final full-strength coat was rubbed with paste wax and extra-fine steel wool.

The design options for this project are numerous. I've mentioned a few with regards to trim style and fluted stiles. But there are the more common changes such as width and height variations to suit your needs. If you plan on loading the shelves with extra-heavy items, add a hardwood strip on the back edge.

Veneer plywood is an excellent choice for this project because of its strength. MDF and solid wood panels are also worth considering.

This bookcase is a simple project and will be one of the most appreciated in your home office.

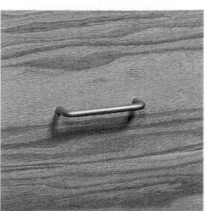

chapter ten

lateral File Cabinet

This lateral file cabinet has two drawers that have been sized to store legal file folders, but they can be reduced in depth if you need to store letter-sized folders instead. It will be used in a home office setting with the executive work center in chapter six and the credenza and bookcase hutch in chapter seven. I've used the same simple finish on all three pieces — three coats of oil-based polyurethane.

Since I plan on using hanging file folders, I've come up with a simple track system using aluminum flat stock. You can use a commercial version, but I've found the flat stock setup to be stronger and less expensive.

The small base raises the cabinet off the floor. For most rooms, this will work fine. However, since there's a heating vent where I want to place my cabinet, I added four wheels. Your cabinet can be built either way. In fact, you can eliminate the 1½"-high base completely and attach the wheels directly to the bottom.

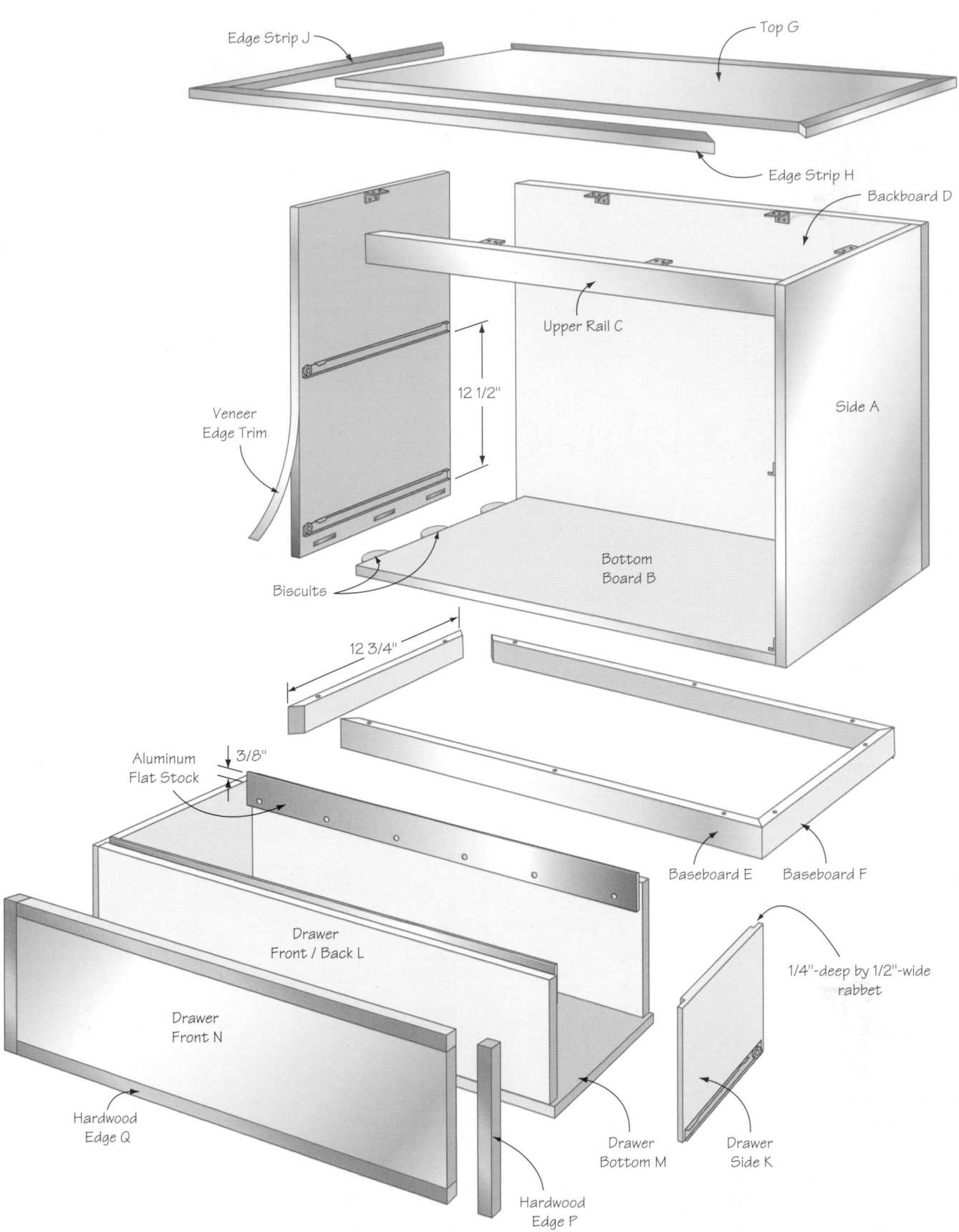

Edge Strip J

Top G

Edge Strip H

Backboard D

Upper Rail C

Side A

Veneer
Edge Trim

12 1/2"

Biscuits

Bottom
Board B

12 3/4"

Aluminum
Flat Stock

3/8"

Baseboard E

Baseboard F

Drawer
Front / Back L

1/4"-deep by 1/2"-wide
rabbet

Drawer
Front N

Hardwood
Edge Q

Drawer
Bottom M

Drawer
Side K

Hardwood
Edge P

Cutting List • Lateral File Cabinet

REF.	QTY.	PART	MATERIAL	THICKNESS	WIDTH	LENGTH	COMMENTS
A	2	Sides	Veneer PB	$^{11}/_{16}$	$16\frac{1}{2}$	$27\frac{3}{4}$	
B	1	Bottom board	Veneer PB	$^{11}/_{16}$	$16\frac{1}{2}$	38	
C	1	Upper rail	Veneer PB	$^{11}/_{16}$	2	38	
D	1	Backboard	Veneer PB	$^{11}/_{16}$	$39\frac{3}{8}$	$27\frac{3}{4}$	
E	2	Baseboards	Solid wood	$\frac{3}{4}$	$1\frac{1}{2}$	$35\frac{1}{4}$	
F	2	Baseboards	Solid wood	$\frac{3}{4}$	$1\frac{1}{2}$	$12\frac{3}{4}$	
G	1	Top	Veneer PB	$^{11}/_{16}$	$15\frac{1}{2}$	38	
H	2	Top edge strips	Solid wood	$\frac{3}{4}$	1	38	
J	2	Top edge strips	Solid wood	$\frac{3}{4}$	1	$15\frac{1}{2}$	

File Drawers

REF.	QTY.	PART	MATERIAL	THICKNESS	WIDTH	LENGTH	COMMENTS
K	4	Sides	Birch ply	$\frac{1}{2}$	10	$16\frac{1}{8}$	
L	4	Front and back	Birch ply	$\frac{1}{2}$	10	$36\frac{1}{2}$	
M	2	Drawer bottom	Birch ply	$\frac{1}{2}$	$16\frac{1}{8}$	37	
N	2	Drawer front	Veneer PB	$^{11}/_{16}$	12	38	
P	4	Drawer edges	Hardwood	$^{11}/_{16}$	$\frac{1}{2}$	12	
Q	4	Drawer edges	Hardwood	$^{11}/_{16}$	$\frac{1}{2}$	39	

Hardware and Supplies

Screws

Full-extension drawer glides

Drawer handles

Wheels (optional)

Nails

Glue

Aluminum flat stock

TIP

These drawers can be quite heavy when fully loaded, so be careful when they're fully open. I plan on securing my cabinet to a wall stud with a 3" screw. You might want to consider doing this as well for an added measure of safety.

Metric Cutting List • Lateral File Cabinet

REF.	QTY.	PART	MATERIAL	THICKNESS	WIDTH	LENGTH	COMMENTS
A	2	Sides	Veneer PB	18	419	705	
B	1	Bottom board	Veneer PB	18	419	965	
C	1	Upper rail	Veneer PB	18	51	965	
D	1	Backboard	Veneer PB	18	1001	705	
E	2	Baseboards	Solid wood	19	38	895	
F	2	Baseboards	Solid wood	19	38	324	
G	1	Top	Veneer PB	18	394	965	
H	2	Top edge strips	Solid wood	19	25	965	
J	2	Top edge strips	Solid wood	19	25	394	

File Drawers

REF.	QTY.	PART	MATERIAL	THICKNESS	WIDTH	LENGTH	COMMENTS
K	4	Sides	Birch ply	13	254	409	
L	4	Front and back	Birch ply	13	254	927	
M	2	Drawer bottom	Birch ply	13	409	940	
N	2	Drawer front	Veneer PB	18	305	965	
P	4	Drawer edges	Hardwood	18	13	305	
Q	4	Drawer edges	Hardwood	18	13	991	

[1] Cut the two sides (A) and apply wood veneer iron-on edge tape to one long edge on each panel. These finished edges will be the fronts.

[2] The bottom board (B) also requires one long edge be taped. Trimming some wood veneers, such as oak, can be difficult. The wood grain is wide and the tape can split along the fibers. To prevent this, use a router equipped with a flush-trim bit. Be sure to hold the router flat on the board and the edge will be perfect.

[3] The sides are joined to the bottom board using glue and screws, dowels or biscuits. I've decided to use biscuits for my project.

[4] Tape one long edge on the upper rail. This will be the downside or exposed edge of the rail. It's attached with glue and a right-angle bracket on each end. The rail face is flush with the outside edges of the sides and even with their tops.

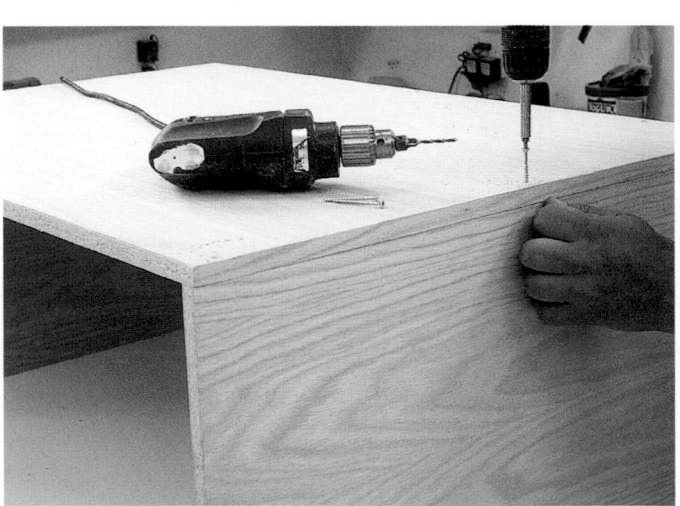

[5] I use a full 11/16"-thick back on this cabinet because of the potential weight in the drawer. Before installing, tape the two outside vertical edges with veneer tape. The back is applied with glue and screws, dowels or biscuits. I am using screws because the back will be against a wall and therefore not visible. If the back of your cabinet is exposed, use dowels or biscuits and glue. You can use screws but the holes must be counterbored and filled with wood plugs or buttons.

TIP

For projects using 11/16" or 3/4" sheet goods, which are to be joined with biscuits, I always use a No. 10 biscuit. The No. 20 setting may cut too deep and there is a possibility the outside of the board can be punctured.

[6] Construct the base with 1x2 solid wood. The corners are mitered at 45° and secured with glue and brad nails.

[7] Clamp the base in place on the underside of the bottom board. It should be 2" in from all edges of the cabinet. Trace its position and drill holes through the bottom board. Apply glue to the base and set the frame in place. Using the previously drilled holes as references, drill pilot holes into the base from the top side of the bottom board. Secure the frame to the bottom board with two 1½" screws on the back, front and two sides.

[8] The top is made with an ¹¹⁄₁₆"-thick veneer PB center and framed with 1½"-wide hardwood. The hardwood frame measurements are given for the inside-to-inside 45°-angled cut on each piece.

[9] Secure the wood edge strips to the top board using No. 20 biscuits and glue. After checking the fit, cutting the biscuit slots and applying glue, clamp the assembly together until the adhesive sets.

[10] Sand the top smooth, being careful not to damage the veneer layer. Round over the top and bottom edges with a ⅜" roundover bit.

[11] Install right-angle brackets on the top edge of the cabinet. These will be used to secure the top board with ⅝" screws.

[12] Clamp the top in place so it's flush with the backboard and equally overhanging on each side. Use ⅝" screws through the brackets into the underside of the top.

[13] Cut the drawer boards using ½"-thick Baltic birch plywood. Glue and nail the sides to the front board and backboard.

[14] The drawer bottoms are attached in the same manner. Take the time to cut each bottom board square. Attaching a board with 90° angles to a box will force it into square.

[15] The 16" drawer glides should be the full-extension type so files can be easily and fully accessed. Side-mounted glides from Accuride or bottom-mounted hardware from Blum are two examples of the hardware I use. Install the glides according to the manufacturer's instructions, leaving a 2" space between the top edge of the bottom drawer and the bottom of the top drawer.

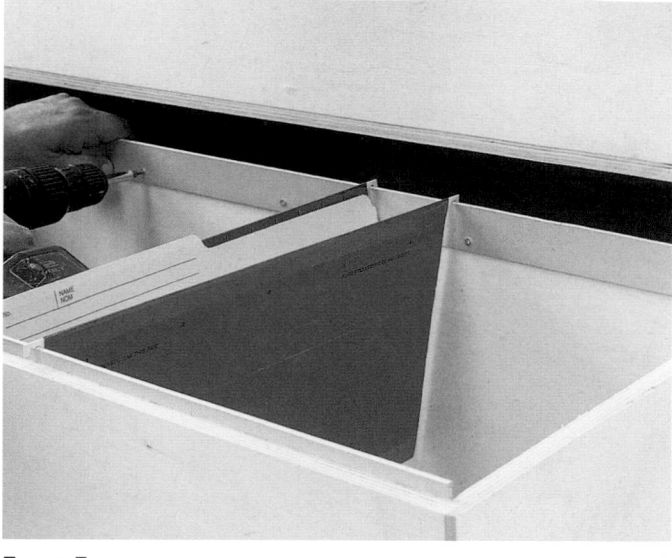

[16] Install a 36"-long by 1½"-wide by ⅛"-thick piece of aluminum flat stock on the inside of each front and back drawer board. This flat stock can be purchased at most hardware stores. The metal is secured with ⅜"-long screws in countersunk holes drilled in the flat stock. Each strip should be ⅜" above the drawer edge so the hanging folders can slide freely along the track.

[17] Glue and nail the hardwood edge strips for the drawer faces in place. I used simple butt joints at each corner; however, they can be cut at 45° to match the top if you wish. Then sand the faces smooth, taking care not to sand through the wood veneer. Use a ⅜" roundover bit to soften the outside edges on each drawer face. Locate and drill the drawer handle holes in the drawer face only. Align the bottom drawer face flush with the underside of the bottom board. Use 2" screws driven through the handle holes into the drawer box to secure the face temporarily. Open the drawer and drive a 1" screw into the drawer face from the inside of the drawer box at each corner. Finally, remove the screws in the handle holes and complete the drilling so the handles can be installed. Repeat the process for the top drawer face, leaving ¹⁄₁₆" between the two faces.

[Construction Notes]

As mentioned in the introduction, I finished my cabinet with three coats of oil-based polyurethane. However, the veneers and solid wood will look great with a stain or water-based clear coat. If you plan on painting your file cabinet, consider using the less expensive poplar veneers and solid wood or MDF.

The wood-edged top and drawer faces are another area that can be modified. Use the wood-edged laminate method, such as was detailed in chapter two, if you want a unique pattern. The GP laminates are very tough and will stand up to more abuse than wood veneers.

You can also opt for a solid wood top. They are made by edge gluing boards, using biscuits. The solid wood tops are beautiful and durable.

The cabinet width, as well as its height and number of drawers, are easily modified to suit your needs. If you have different subjects in your file system, you may want three 24"-wide drawers to better separate the information. The construction methods are the same no matter what design you choose.

The hanging file folders I found in my local stationery store appeared to be all the same width. However, before building the cabinet I suggest you check the folders in your area. I don't suspect they would be different but it's worth the time to be sure.

And finally, the cabinet can be mounted on the 1½"-high base or on wheels as I mentioned in the introduction. The base height is variable and doesn't affect any other dimension. If you live in an older home with high baseboards, you might want to alter the size. If the baseboard frame clears the trim it will allow the cabinet to sit tightly against a wall. By doing that, the cabinet-to-wall gap is eliminated and you won't have papers falling off the back.

chapter eleven

media Storage Center

This project is designed to hold and organize all of your media — including computer disks, CDs, audio tapes and videotapes. There is a section for books with an adjustable shelf and two drawers for all the other media forms. The drawers have movable partitions that will allow you to customize each one to your specific needs. I will be using the top drawer for CD storage because most of the data and software I buy is in this form.

This storage center will hold a great deal of material and should meet the most demanding requirements. But if you do run out of space, build another unit. It's not that expensive and is well worth the investment. All your reference data in one location, easily indexed and accessible, will save you money and, more importantly, valuable time.

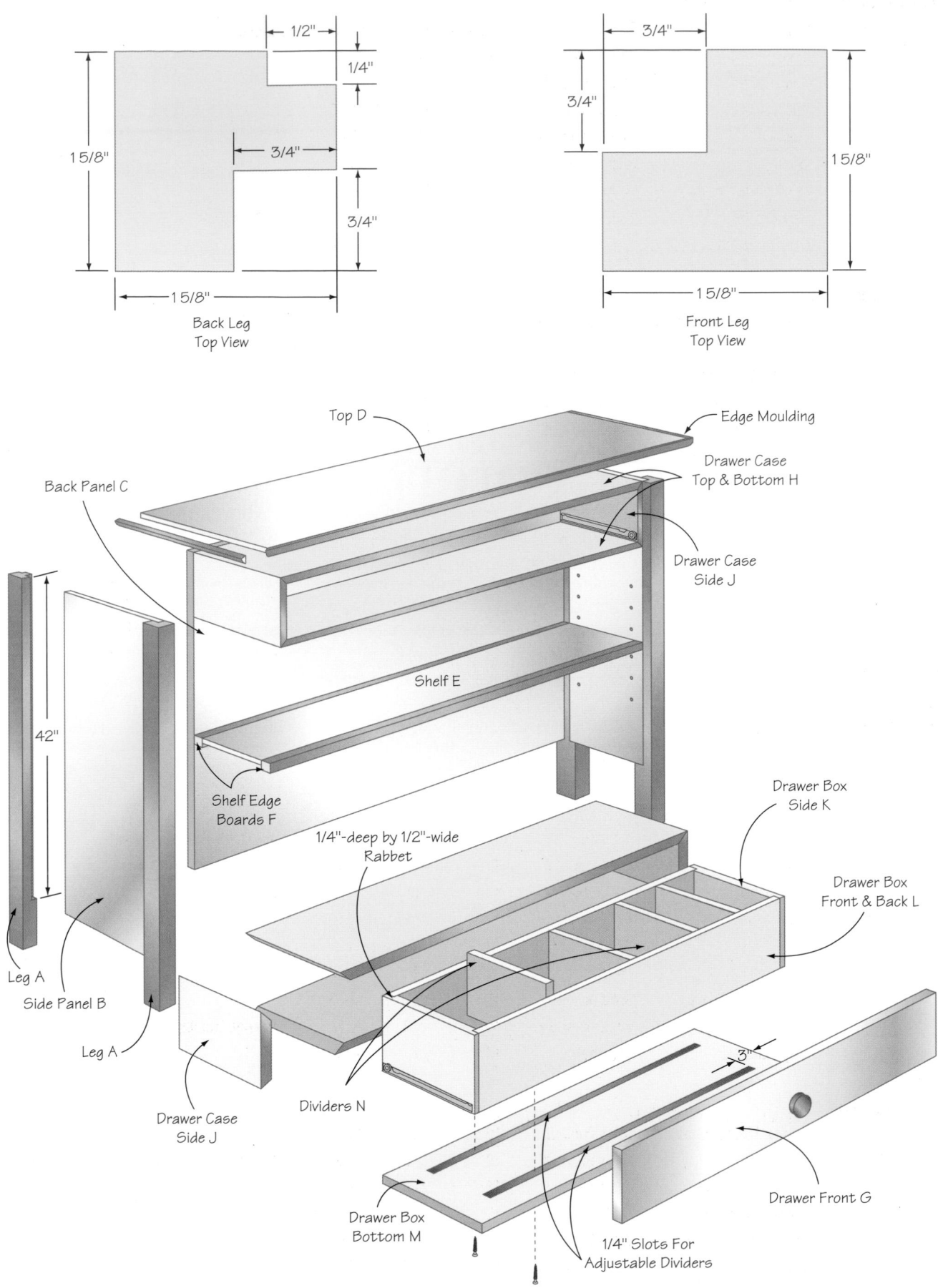

1/2"
1/4"
3/4"
15/8"
3/4"
15/8"
Back Leg
Top View

3/4"
3/4"
15/8"
15/8"
Front Leg
Top View

Top D
Edge Moulding
Drawer Case
Top & Bottom H
Back Panel C
Drawer Case
Side J
42"
Shelf E
Drawer Box
Side K
Shelf Edge
Boards F
1/4"-deep by 1/2"-wide
Rabbet
Drawer Box
Front & Back L
Leg A
Side Panel B
Leg A
Dividers N
Drawer Case
Side J
3"
Drawer Box
Bottom M
Drawer Front G
1/4" Slots For
Adjustable Dividers

Cutting List • Media Storage Center

REF.	QTY.	PART	MATERIAL	THICKNESS	WIDTH	LENGTH	COMMENTS
A	4	Legs	Solid oak	1⅝	1⅝	47¾	
B	2	Side panels	Oak veneer ply	¾	11¾	42	
C	1	Back panel	Oak veneer ply	¼	43	42	
D	1	Top	Oak veneer ply	¾	13½	47¼	
E	1	Shelf	Oak veneer ply	¾	11	41⅞	
F	2	Shelf edge boards	Solid oak	¾	1½	41⅞	
G	2	Drawer fronts	Oak veneer ply	¾	8	41¾	With edge banding
	1	Edge moulding	Solid oak	¾	¾	8 feet	
Drawer Case & Drawer Boxes							
H	4	Top and bottom boards	Oak veneer ply	¾	12⅜	42	Cut at 45°
J	4	Sides	Oak veneer ply	¾	12⅜	8½	Cut at 45°
K	4	Drawer box sides	Baltic birch ply	½	5	12	
L	4	Fronts and backs	Baltic birch ply	½	5	39	
M	2	Drawer box bottoms	Baltic birch ply	½	12	39½	
N	10	Dividers	Baltic birch ply	½	5	11	

Hardware and Supplies

- Screws
- Nails
- Glue
- Biscuits or dowels
- Three-quarter extension drawer glides
- 107° hidden hinges
- Commercial CD racks (optional)
- Drawer and door handles

Metric Cutting List • Media Storage Center

REF.	QTY.	PART	MATERIAL	THICKNESS	WIDTH	LENGTH	COMMENTS
A	4	Legs	Solid oak	41	41	1213	
B	2	Side panels	Oak veneer ply	19	298	1067	
C	1	Back panel	Oak veneer ply	6	1092	1067	
D	1	Top	Oak veneer ply	19	343	1200	
E	1	Shelf	Oak veneer ply	19	279	1063	
F	2	Shelf edge boards	Solid oak	19	38	1063	
G	2	Drawer fronts	Oak veneer ply	19	203	1060	With edge banding
	1	Edge moulding	Solid oak	19	19	2438	
Drawer Case & Drawer Boxes							
H	4	Top and bottom boards	Oak veneer ply	19	315	1067	Cut at 45°
J	4	Sides	Oak veneer ply	19	315	216	Cut at 45°
K	4	Drawer box sides	Baltic birch ply	13	127	305	
L	4	Fronts and backs	Baltic birch ply	13	127	991	
M	2	Drawer box bottoms	Baltic birch ply	13	305	1004	
N	10	Dividers	Baltic birch ply	13	127	279	

[1] Prepare the four legs by cutting them to length. Each leg needs a ¾"-wide by ¾"-deep rabbet (that's 42" long measured from the top) formed on one corner. These rabbets will receive the side panels so orient them properly as two mirror-image sets. Check the drawing and mark the legs before cutting the rabbet to avoid mistakes. Use a ¾" straight-cutting router bit. Once the cut has been completed, square the bottom with a chisel.

[2] The back legs require a ¼"-deep by ½"-wide by 42"-long second rabbet measured from the top of the leg cut to receive the ¼" backboard.

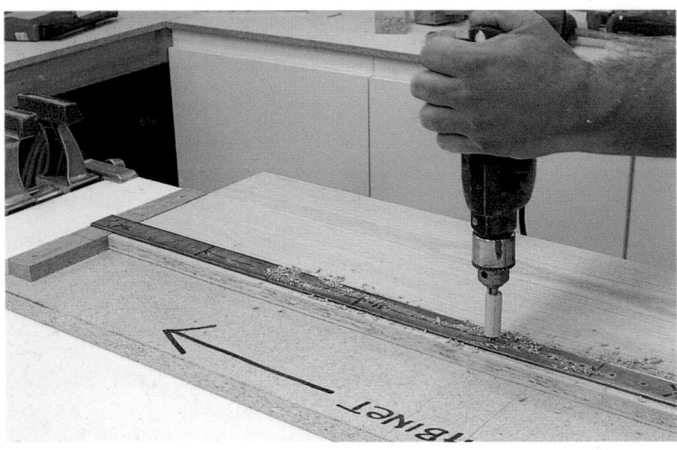

[3] Cut the side panels (B) and drill holes for the adjustable shelf pins. The holes are spaced about 1¼" apart and are 1" in from each side. Two rows of holes per panel are required. Begin the rows of holes 10" from the top and bottom of each panel on the inside face.

[4] Assemble both sides with glue and clamps. The panels are installed in the ¾"-square rabbet and should be flush with the inside face of each leg set. Be certain the pin holes are aligned correctly and the back panel rabbets are located properly. Drive 1¼" screws through the panel, into each leg, at the top and bottom.

TIP

You can also cut rabbets on a table saw with two right-angle cuts. Stop short of making a full-length cut because the curve of the blade will run past your stop line. Use a sharp chisel to remove the remaining waste and complete the rabbet.

[5] When the adhesive has set, sand both assemblies and round over the exposed corners of each leg. Use a ⅜" roundover bit in a router.

[7] Assemble both cases with glue on the miters and 2" screws. It's always good practice to drill a pilot hole for the screws. Two screws per joint will lock them securely. They won't be seen, so we don't have to cover the screw heads.

[6] Square cut all the drawer case pieces a little longer than required. Apply wood veneer edge tape to the front edge of all eight boards. Then cut both ends at 45° to the dimension detailed in the cutting list. You will be cutting the edge tape at the same time and the result will be a clean angled edge. Note that all drawer case measurements given are at the longest part of the miter.

[8] Attach the two cases to both end assemblies. The upper case is flush with the top of the legs. And the lower case is flush with the side panel bottom edges. Use glue and 2"-long screws to secure the cases. Drive the screws through the inside face of each side board into the legs. The cases are installed ¼" ahead of the rear face of each leg. This will allow us to fit the backboard in the rabbets, tightly against the back edge of each case.

[9] The back panel (C) is installed in the rabbets. Apply glue to the rabbets as well as the back edges of each case and nail the panel in place. I saved a little money by using three cutoff panels I had in the shop. I joined the panels along the horizontal boards of each case so the joint wouldn't be seen from the front. You can use a full panel or make use of smaller pieces in your shop.

[10] The top (D) is attached with glue and eight 1¼" screws. Drive the screws through the underside of the upper case top board.

[11] Choose a ¾"-wide moulding or make your own, and attach it to the front and both sides of the top. Miter the corners at 45°, securing the moulding with glue and brad nails. Fill the nail holes with wood putty.

[12] Cut the shelf board and the two edge boards (F). Attach the edges on the front and back using glue and biscuits, screws with wood plugs, or nails. Ease the top and bottom corners on the front edge piece with a ⅜" roundover bit. These hardwood edges add strength to this long shelf and increase its load capacity.

[13] The overall size of both drawer boxes is 5½"-high by 12"-deep and 39½"-wide, or 1" less in width than the inside dimension of the drawer case. This 1" clearance is needed for the full-extension glides. Cut all the boards for both drawer boxes. The four sides (K) need a ¼"-deep by ½"-wide rabbet on each inside edge. Build the box by attaching the front and back boards to the side rabbets with glue and brad nails.

[14] Install the bottom using glue and ¾" brad nails. Remember, an accurately cut bottom board will square the drawer box.

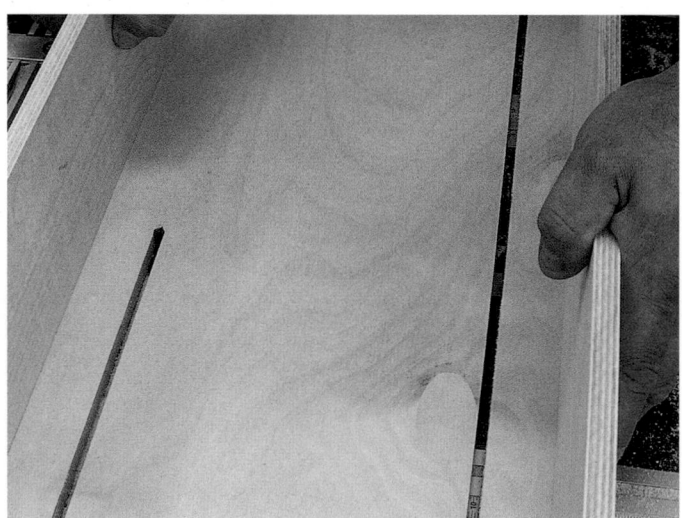

[15] Form the two slots in each drawer box with a ¼" straight router bit. The slots run parallel to the front and back board. Locate them 1½" in from the front and back, and end them 3" from the side boards.

[16] Drill two pilot holes in the bottom of each divider to match the slot spacing. Use 1½" screws and washers to secure the dividers. They can be positioned, or moved at a later date, to meet your specific requirements.

[17] The drawers are installed using 12" full-extension drawer glides. Be sure the drawer box is positioned far enough above the drawer case bottom to provide proper clearance for the divider screws.

[18] My drawer fronts, made with ¾" plywood veneer, have edges covered with wood tape. However, you can use a five-piece face, solid wood, or dress up the plywood veneer face with moulding. Use four 1" screws driven into the back of each drawer face through the box front board.

[Construction Notes]

I completed my media storage center by installing solid wood knobs. Three coats of polyurethane, the first coat cut by 10 percent with thinners, and sanding between each coat will protect my project.

As I've often stated in this book, the choice of materials and finish is a matter of personal taste. Often, other furnishings in the room will dictate the choice.

The height of this project was determined by the media to be stored.

The drawers were designed to hold CDs, and I wanted a bookcase with shelf height to accommodate large books and binders. The width can be varied to suit your space requirements. Making the center narrower isn't a problem; however, if you do need more width, it may be wise to build two units. Drawer and shelf width is at the practical maximum with this design.

Using veneer PB or MDF and paint can reduce the cost of this project. The drawer glides can be replaced with standard three-quarter extension glides. However, access to the drawer is improved with the full-extension glides and you'll be pleased you've spent the extra money.

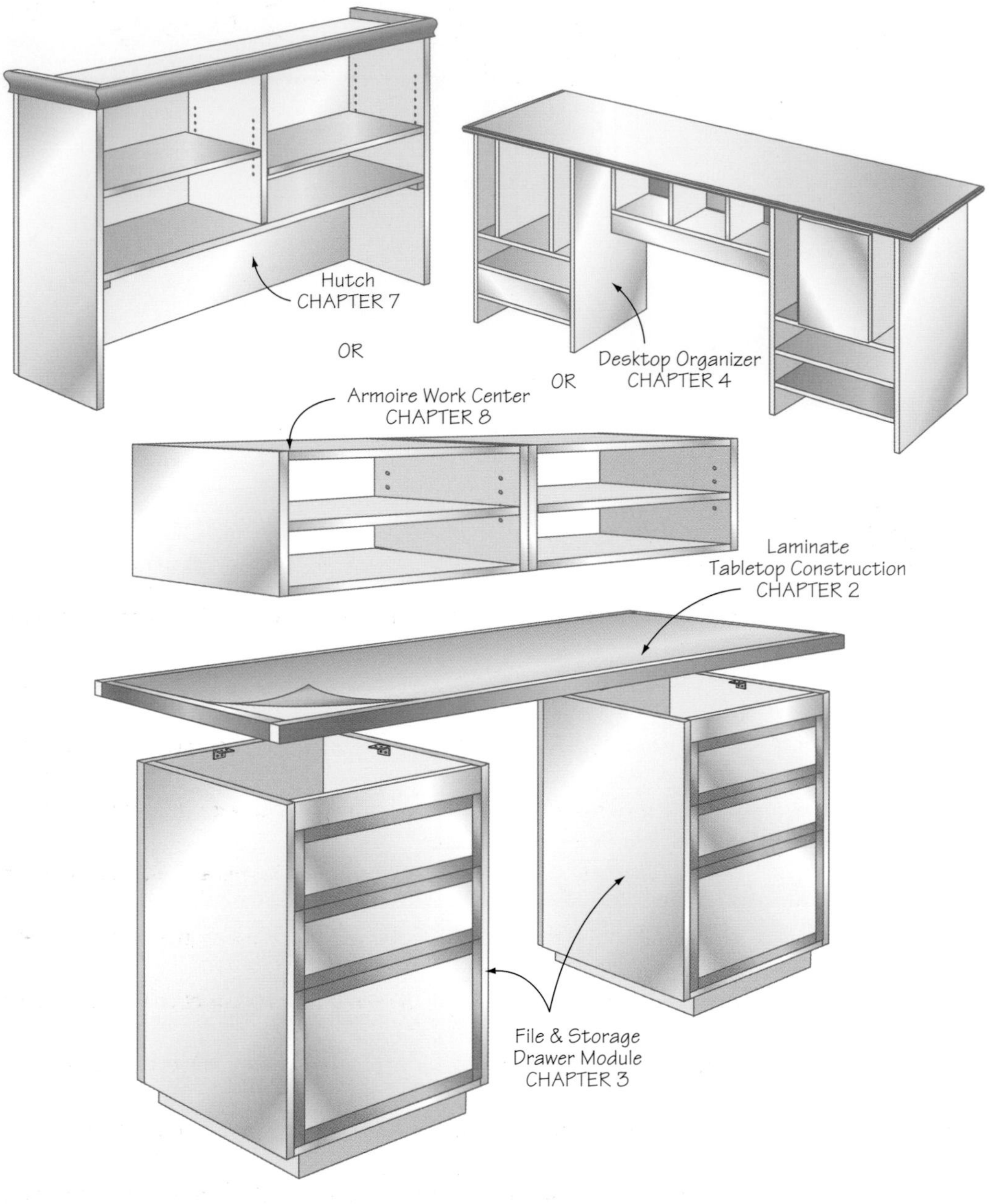

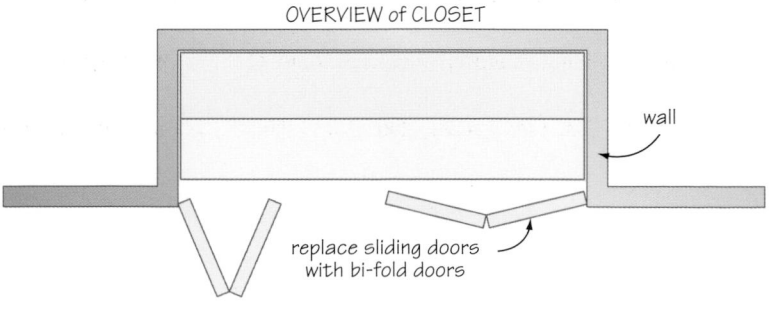

Hutch
CHAPTER 7

OR

Desktop Organizer
CHAPTER 4

OR

Armoire Work Center
CHAPTER 8

Laminate
Tabletop Construction
CHAPTER 2

File & Storage
Drawer Module
CHAPTER 3

OVERVIEW of CLOSET

wall

replace sliding doors
with bi-fold doors

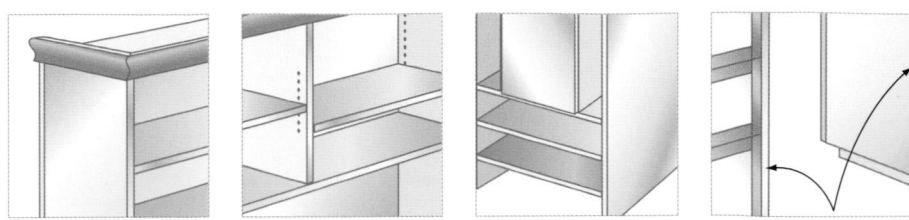

closet Work Center

Many of us have closets in our homes that collect junk. Space is always at a premium in any house, so turning a closet into a functional home office makes a great deal of sense. However, all closets are different, so providing you with specific dimensions isn't possible. I can illustrate a number of options using the projects already detailed in this book.

The first place to start is to decide how to hide the office space when it's not being used. Sliding doors are very common on closets, but aren't much good for a work center. The perfect solution is bi-fold doors. They are easy to install because most are sold as a kit with all the necessary hardware. Fortunately, there are a lot of choices and the cost is reasonable.

Study the illustration at the left with your closet space dimensions in mind and decide which projects you want. Some closets aren't very wide and you may be restricted to one drawer module and tabletop, with a simple bookcase above. If you're lucky and have 6' or more, you can install many of the suggested options.

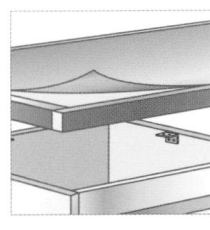

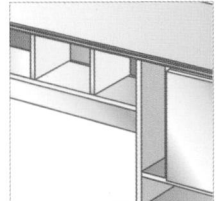

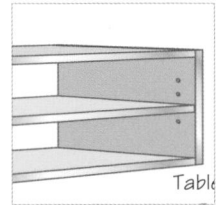

Tabl

A tower utilizes all the space and it is easy to build. Extend the side panels of the drawer modules in chapter three and add a door with shelves. The upper section can be used to store stationery supplies and media disks by adding a couple of adjustable shelves.

Wood-edged countertops, which are detailed in chapter two, can be made to custom fit any space. And there are dozens of pattern choices available.

MPB is an inexpensive option to consider when choosing your sheet material. It's stable and strong when used correctly. Apply iron-on edge tape and you have finished panels ready for assembly.

Base cabinets, using ⅝"-thick MPB, are constructed using the techniques in chapter three. Upper cabinets have one extra board for the top. All the pieces, including the backboard, are ⅝"-thick PB and joined with PB screws in piloted holes.

Inexpensive drawers can be made with MPB using a full-thickness bottom. They are built in the same manner as the Baltic birch drawers, without the side rabbets. They are strong, easy to maintain and simple to install on bottom-mounted drawer glides.

MPB sheets come in dozens of colors and simulated woodgrain finishes. Many manufacturers can also supply a matching edge tape.

Cabinet doors and drawer faces are low-cost alternatives for the closet work center cabinets. Cut the boards to size, tape the edges and install.

Closet work centers can be enhanced with divider panels for shelf support. One big advantage in these spaces is the ability to anchor partitions to the floor with metal brackets.

Hang wall cabinets in your closet work space using 3" screws driven into the studs. The two side walls and back wall allow us to install all types of cabinets and bookcase storage units.

Don't overlook lighting requirements when converting your closet into a work center. Fluorescent fixtures are ideal and the looks can be improved upon with a few boards and a sheet of ⅛"-thick Plexiglas. Build a box using 1x6 material, add moulding to the bottom edge that's wide enough to create a ¼"-wide inside lip, and slip in the Plexiglas panel.

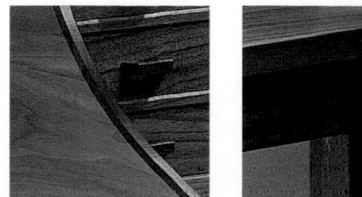

chapter thirteen

writing Desk

Sometimes you need a quiet place to sit and write that letter or novel. This desk is based on the style of a rolltop desk. It gives the feeling of privacy with the wrap-around sides and has plenty of drawers and cubbyholes to keep things organized. The faux leather top creates a perfect writing surface. The top also opens up to reveal a pencil holder and room for storing writing paper inside.

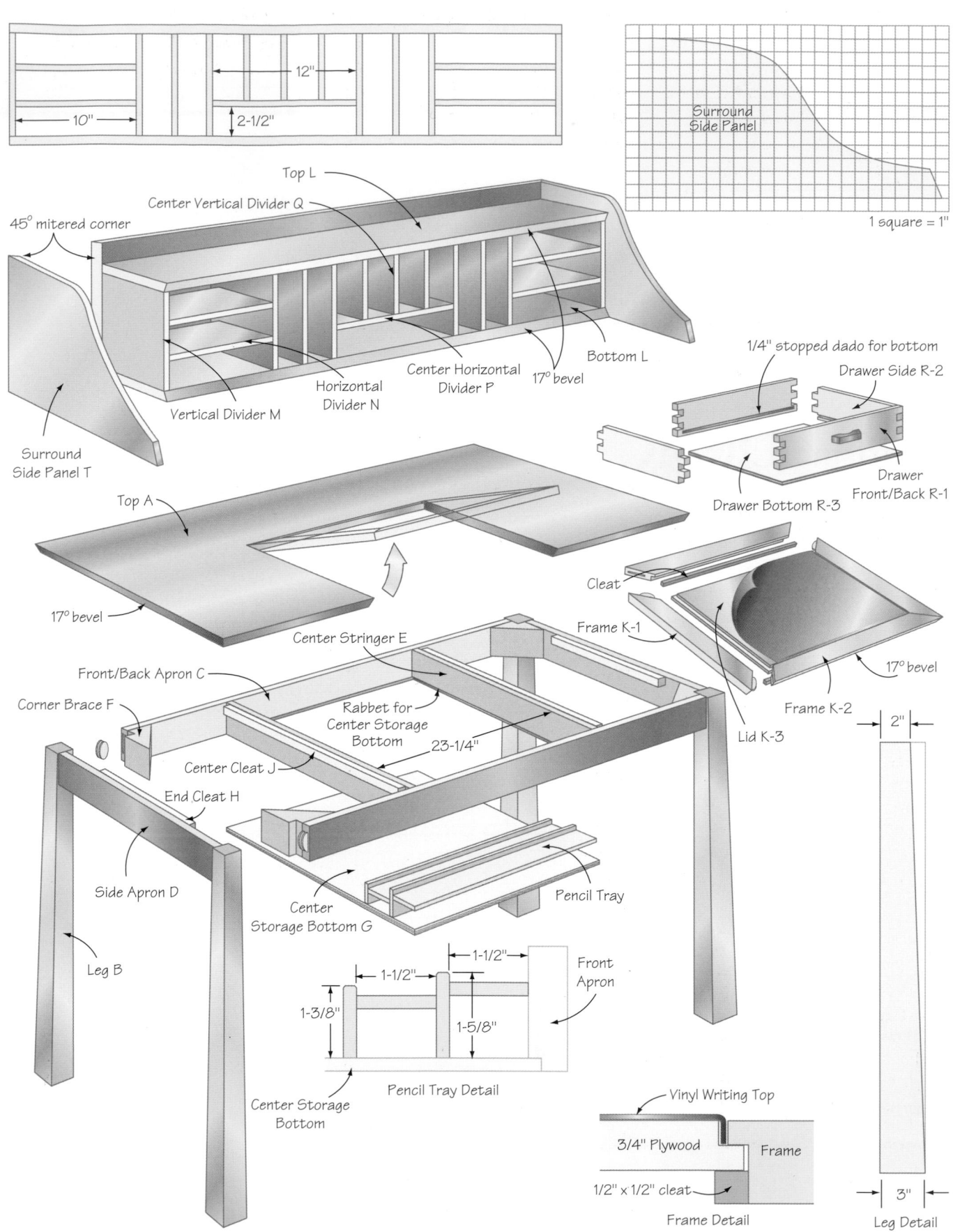

12"

10"

2-1/2"

Surround Side Panel

1 square = 1"

Top L

Center Vertical Divider Q

45° mitered corner

1/4" stopped dado for bottom

Drawer Side R-2

Bottom L

17° bevel

Center Horizontal Divider P

Horizontal Divider N

Vertical Divider M

Drawer Front/Back R-1

Surround Side Panel T

Drawer Bottom R-3

Top A

Cleat

17° bevel

Frame K-1

17° bevel

Center Stringer E

Frame K-2

Lid K-3

Front/Back Apron C

Rabbet for Center Storage Bottom

2"

Corner Brace F

Center Cleat J

23-1/4"

End Cleat H

Side Apron D

Center Storage Bottom G

Pencil Tray

Leg B

1-1/2"

1-1/2"

Front Apron

1-3/8"

1-5/8"

Center Storage Bottom

Pencil Tray Detail

Vinyl Writing Top

3/4" Plywood

Frame

1/2" x 1/2" cleat

Frame Detail

3"

Leg Detail

Cutting List • Writing Desk

REF.	QTY.	PART	MATERIAL	THICKNESS	WIDTH	LENGTH	COMMENTS
A	1	Top	Walnut	1¼	28	48	w/24"-wide by 18"-deep lid opening
B	4	Legs*	Walnut	3	3	28½	Each leg tapers to 2" at the top
C	2	Front and back aprons	Walnut	⅞	3	41½	
D	2	Side aprons	Walnut	⅞	3	21½	
E	2	Center stringers	Walnut	¾	3	23¾	
F	4	Corner braces	Walnut	1¾	3	5	
G	1	Center storage bottom	Birch ply	½	24	24½	
H	2	End cleats	Poplar	⅞	⅞	15½	
J	2	Center cleats	Poplar	⅞	⅞	23½	
K	1	Lid	Walnut	1¼	17⅞	2315/16	
K-1	2	Lid frame sides	Walnut	1¼	1½	17⅞	
K-2	2	Lid frame top & bottom	Walnut	1¼	1½	23 15/16	
K-3	1	Lid panel	Walnut	¾	16⅜	22 7/16	

*Note: The legs are tapered on the two outside sides only. The inside sides are left square for ease of assembly.

Cutting List • Desktop Organizer for the Writing Desk

REF.	QTY.	PART	MATERIAL	THICKNESS	WIDTH	LENGTH	COMMENTS
L	2	Top and bottom	Walnut	¾	8	45¾	
M	8	Vertical dividers	Walnut	½	7½	8½	
N	4	Horizontal dividers	Walnut	½	7½	10	
P	1	Center horizontal divider	Walnut	½	7½	12	
Q	3	Center vertical dividers	Walnut	½	7½	5½	
R	6	Drawers	Walnut	2½ high	10	7⅜ deep	
R-1	6	Fronts and backs	Walnut	½	2½	9 9/16	
R-2	12	Sides	Walnut	½	2½	7⅜	
R-3	6	Bottoms	Walnut	¼	6 13/16	9½	
S	1	Surround back	Walnut	¾	12	47¼	
T	2	Surround side panels	Walnut	¾	12	22½	
U	2	Pencil tray bottoms	Walnut	¼	1½	23¼	
V	1	Pencil tray front	Walnut	¼	1⅜	23¼	
W	1	Pencil tray center	Walnut	¼	1⅝	23¼	
X	6	Drawer pulls	Padauk	½	¾	2	Any contrasting wood will work

Hardware and Supplies

Vinyl writing top 1/16" x 17½" x 23½" (1.5mm x 445mm x 597mm)

18mm Soss hinges (2)

Screws

Glue

Biscuits

Contact cement

Metric Cutting List • Writing Desk

REF.	QTY.	PART	MATERIAL	THICKNESS	WIDTH	LENGTH	COMMENTS
A	1	Top	Walnut	32	711	1219	w/610mm-wide by 457mm-deep lid opening
B	4	Legs*	Walnut	76	76	724	Each leg tapers to 51mm at the top
C	2	Front and back aprons	Walnut	22	76	1054	
D	2	Side aprons	Walnut	22	76	546	
E	2	Center stringers	Walnut	19	76	603	
F	4	Corner braces	Walnut	45	76	127	
G	1	Center storage bottom	Birch ply	13	610	623	
H	2	End cleats	Poplar	22	22	394	
J	2	Center cleats	Poplar	22	22	597	
K	1	Lid	Walnut	32	454	608	
K-1	2	Lid frame sides	Walnut	32	38	454	
K-2	2	Lid frame top & bottom	Walnut	32	38	608	
K-3	1	Lid panel	Walnut	19	416	570	

*Note: The legs are tapered on the two outside sides only. The inside sides are left square for ease of assembly.

Metric Cutting List • Desktop Organizer for the Writing Desk

REF.	QTY.	PART	MATERIAL	THICKNESS	WIDTH	LENGTH	COMMENTS
L	2	Top and bottom	Walnut	19	203	1162	
M	8	Vertical dividers	Walnut	13	191	216	
N	4	Horizontal dividers	Walnut	13	191	254	
P	1	Center horizontal divider	Walnut	13	191	305	
Q	3	Center vertical dividers	Walnut	13	191	140	
R	6	Drawers	Walnut	64 high	254	188 deep	
R-1	6	Fronts and backs	Walnut	13	64	243	
R-2	12	Sides	Walnut	13	64	188	
R-3	6	Bottoms	Walnut	6	173	242	
S	1	Surround back	Walnut	19	305	1200	
T	2	Surround side panels	Walnut	19	305	572	
U	2	Pencil tray bottoms	Walnut	6	38	590	
V	1	Pencil tray front	Walnut	6	35	590	
W	1	Pencil tray center	Walnut	6	41	590	
X	6	Drawer pulls	Padauk	13	19	51	Any contrasting wood will work

[1] Use a tapering jig to put the taper on the legs. This homemade jig can be adjusted to make a variety of tapers. (Note the two adjusting screws that make it easy to change the amount of taper.)

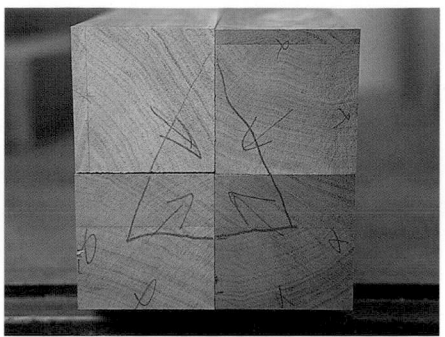

[2] Mark the tops of the legs with an orienting triangle. This is a great aid in keeping the legs in proper order.

[3] Using double biscuits increases the joint strength significantly.

[4] After routing a small bevel on the bottom outside edge of the aprons. Glue up the assembly of the two long apron pieces and the two stringers.

[5] Cut a rabbet in the glued-up assembly for the bottom piece of the storage area.

[6] Glue the two end apron/leg assemblies together first. Then glue the two end assemblies together. Use the scrap wedge-shaped pieces that fell off when cutting the leg tapers as shims to square the clamp faces to the assembly.

[7] After cutting the corner blocks to size on a miter saw, go to the table saw and cut notches in the corner blocks for the legs. This can also be done either with a handsaw or on the band saw.

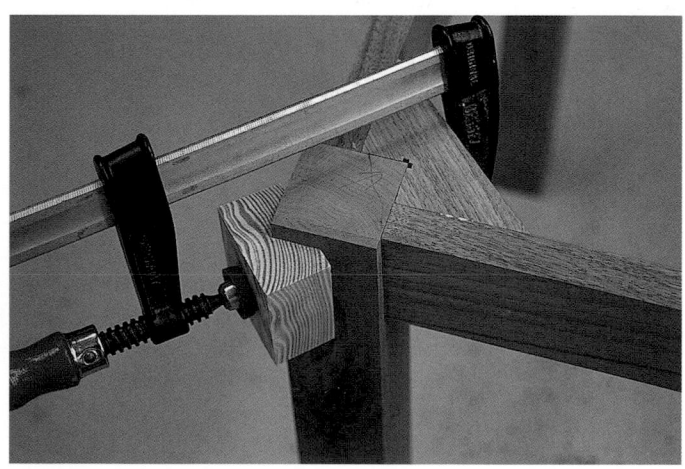

[8] Glue the corner blocks in place. These blocks add strength to the leg/apron corner assemblies.

[9] After gluing cleats to the aprons and stringers for attaching the top to the base, drill ¼" pilot holes in the cleats for screwing the top to the base. These oversize holes will let the screws move with the solid wood top.

[10] Make the top in three pieces (this makes it easy to create the opening for the lid). Double-check for squareness. Cut the angle on the top's edge using a table saw or a circular saw.

[11] Attach the top with washers and screws. The washers help to keep the screws from pulling into the cleats.

TIP

The upper desk organizer has several cubbyholes and six openings for the drawers. Take your time laying out this assembly and draw lines where all the parts will go. Using biscuits to assemble this organizer will make it easier to line everything up at assembly time. By laying the top and bottom out at the same time, it is easy to see where all the parts will go.

[12] Attach the storage area bottom with screws. You can leave the rabbet corners rounded or square them out. Either way will look good.

[13] On a table saw, cut the rabbet on the lid frame stock. Then cut the stock to length as indicated in the cutting list and glue the parts together. Use biscuits in the corner joints for strength.

[14] Cut a ¾" birch (or any smooth veneer) plywood panel to fit exactly in the opening of the desk lid. Then cut a rabbet on all the edges of the panel so it fits into the top frame opening of the lid. Make sure that the top surface of the panel is flush to the top surface of the frame. Allow for the thickness of the faux leather material around the edges of the top opening. Attach the vinyl to the panel with contact cement. Roll it out smoothly, starting in the center of the panel and working out to the edges, so no bubbles occur.

[15] Trim the vinyl so there is a flap left all around the edges of the panel lip. This flap will fold into the opening of the frame when the panel is installed. Cut a notch in the vinyl at the corners so it will fold properly.

[16] The panel can then be pushed into the lid opening from the inside of the frame and the vinyl will fold into the rabbet.

[Cutting Box-Joint Fingers]

After setting up the dado stack cutters to cut a ⅜"-wide by ⅜"-deep notch, make the first cut in the miter-gauge fence. Cut a piece of wood the exact size of the dado cut in the fence and put it in the slot with part of it sticking out past the face of the fence. Move the fence over the exact width of the dado cut. This will give you the proper spacing for cutting the fingers.

[1] Place a spacer the same width of the finger against the spacing block and make the first cut. Note the sandpaper attached to the miter fence to help hold the pieces firmly in place.

[2] Move the piece until the spacing block is in the slot you just cut and make the second cut.

[3] Repeat this step for the final cut.

[4] Place the edge of the side against the spacer block and make the first cut.

[5] Move the side piece over and drop the side over the spacer block into the cut just made and make the final cut.

[6] This is what the assembled joint will look like when all of the fingers are cut.

[17] Secure the panel in place with cleats. The cleats can be removed if the top material needs to be replaced.

[18] Attach the lid to the desk. I used invisible Soss hinges, but a brass continuous hinge would also look great. Finally, sand all the parts, finishing up with 150-grit sandpaper. This project was finished with three coats of catalyzed lacquer. A wipe-on finish containing Danish or tung oil and polyurethane would work very well also. Sand with 320-grit sandpaper between coats. Rub out the final coat with #0000 steel wool.

[19] The desktop organizer is assembled using biscuit joinery. Dry fit the desktop organizer to be sure it will all come together properly. Then glue the two drawer opening sections and the center assembly together first, and then the whole organizer (you may want to finish all the parts first, then glue it all together).

[20] Use cardboard to mock-up the shape of parts so you can see what they will look like. This gives you the freedom to change any shape very easily. Then use the cardboard mock-up as a pattern to make a routing template from ¼" plywood.

[21] When the surround parts are cut, lay the parts flat with the miters facing down. Butt the edges of the miters to each other and tape the joints together using clear packaging tape. Carefully turn the assembly over, apply glue in the miter joint and fold it into a right angle. Stand the surround assembly up and let the glue dry completely before moving it. (You might need to use a large bar clamp at the front edges to pull the assembly square.)

[22] Now it's time to glue up the pencil holder.

[23] Cut a stopped dado for the drawer bottom in the front and back pieces. This dado is cut all the way through on the side pieces.

[24] Fit the drawers with a belt sander.

stand-up Desk

If you think better on your feet, then you definitely need this desk. You can put your foot on the front rail and get really comfortable. The two drawers have pencil holders and plenty of room for paper storage. The top has a faux leather panel that provides a nice writing surface. The stool provides a place to sit if you want to rest your feet.

Many of the techniques used to build this desk are the same as are used to build the walnut writing desk in the previous chapter. Just refer back to that chapter to review any of these techniques.

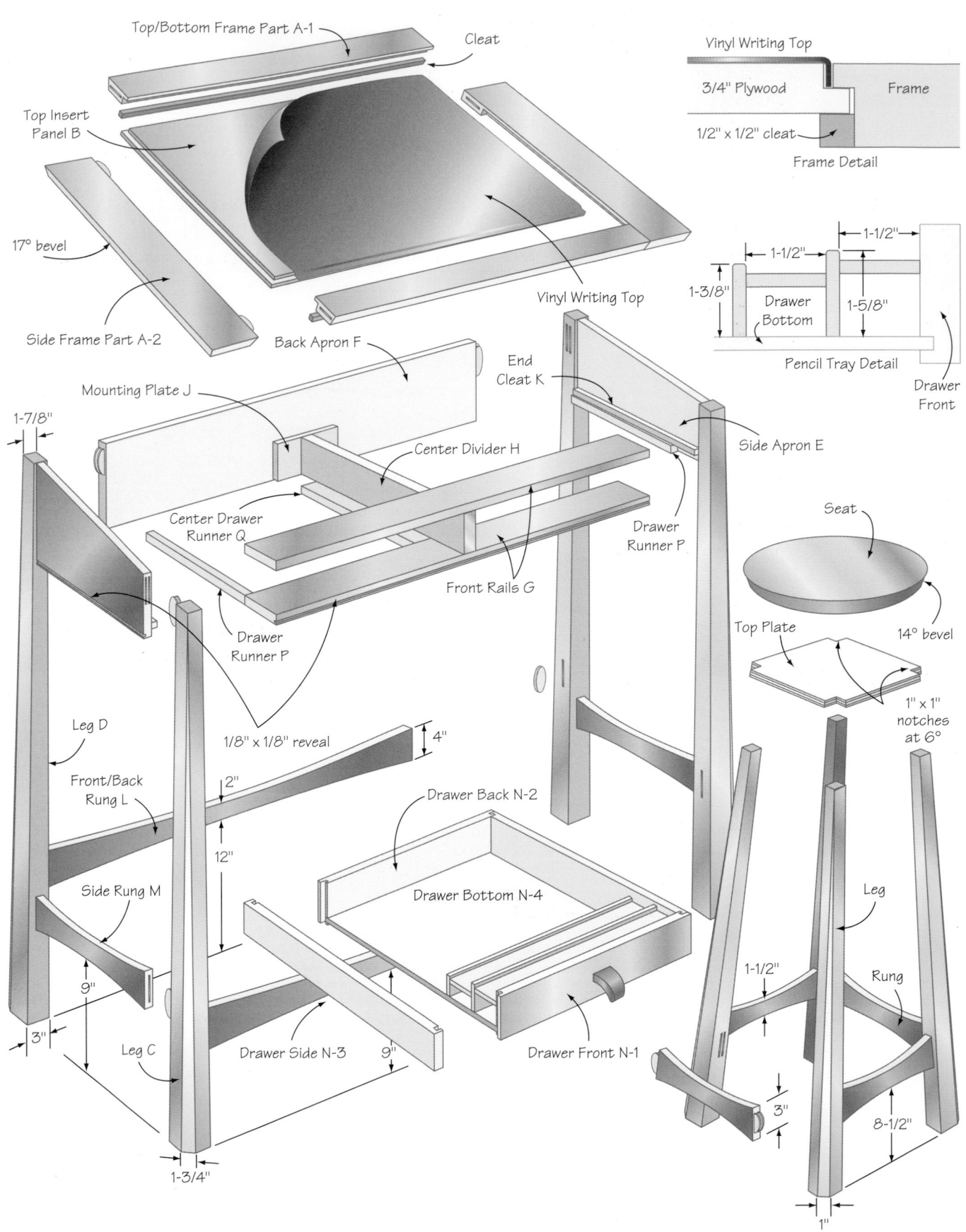

Top/Bottom Frame Part A-1

Cleat

Vinyl Writing Top

3/4" Plywood

Frame

1/2" x 1/2" cleat

Frame Detail

Top Insert Panel B

17° bevel

Side Frame Part A-2

Back Apron F

Vinyl Writing Top

1-1/2"

1-1/2"

1-3/8"

Drawer Bottom

1-5/8"

Pencil Tray Detail

Drawer Front

Mounting Plate J

End Cleat K

Side Apron E

Center Divider H

Center Drawer Runner Q

Drawer Runner P

Seat

Front Rails G

Drawer Runner P

Top Plate

14° bevel

Drawer Runner P

1/8" x 1/8" reveal

4"

1" x 1" notches at 6°

Leg D

2"

Front/Back Rung L

12"

Drawer Back N-2

Drawer Bottom N-4

Leg

Side Rung M

9"

Rung

3"

Leg C

Drawer Side N-3

9"

Drawer Front N-1

1-1/2"

1-3/4"

3"

8-1/2"

1"

Cutting List • Stand-Up Desk

REF.	QTY.	PART	MATERIAL	THICKNESS	WIDTH	LENGTH	COMMENTS
A	1	Top	Ash	1¼	23½	38	
A-1	2	Top/bottom frame parts	Ash	1¼	3	28	
A-2	2	Side frame parts	Ash	1¼	5	23½	
B	1	Top insert panel	Birch ply	¾	18½	29	
C	2	Front legs*	Ash	3	3	42	Each leg tapers to 1⅞" at the top
D	2	Back legs*	Ash	3	3	44	Each leg tapers to 1⅞" at the top
E	2	Side aprons	Ash	1	5-7	17¾	See illustration for details
F	1	Back apron	Ash	1	7	32¼	
G	2	Front rails	Ash	1	4	33¼	See illustration for details
H	1	Center divider	Ash	1	2⅝	19¼	
J	1	Mounting plate	Plywood	¾	3	3	Attach to back end of center divider
K	2	End cleats	Ash	⅞	⅞	17½	
L	2	Front and back rungs	Ash	1	4	32¼	
M	2	Side rungs	Ash	1	4	17¾	
N	2	Drawers	Ash	2⅝	15⅝	19¼	
N-1	2	Fronts	Ash	¾	2⅝	15⅝	
N-2	2	Backs	Ash	½	2⅝	15⅛	
N-3	4	Sides	Ash	½	2⅝	19	
N-4	2	Bottoms	Birch ply	¼	15⅛	18¾	
P	2	Drawer runners	Ash	1	1	15½	
Q	1	Center drawer runner	Ash	1	3	15½	
R	4	Pencil tray bottoms	Ash	¼	1½	23¼	
S	2	Pencil tray front	Ash	¼	1⅜	23¼	
T	2	Pencil tray center	Ash	¼	1⅝	23¼	
U	2	Drawer pulls	Padauk	¾	1	1¼	Any contrasting wood will work; see illustration for details

*Note: The legs are tapered on the two outside sides only. The inside sides are left square for ease of assembly.

Hardware and Supplies

Vinyl writing top 1/16" x 20" x 30½"

Screws

Glue

Biscuits

Contact cement

Metric Cutting List • Stand-Up Desk

REF.	QTY.	PART	MATERIAL	THICKNESS	WIDTH	LENGTH	COMMENTS
A	1	Top	Ash	32	597	965	
A-1	2	Top/bottom frame parts	Ash	32	76	711	
A-2	2	Side frame parts	Ash	32	127	597	
B	1	Top insert panel	Birch ply	19	470	737	
C	2	Front legs*	Ash	76	76	1067	Each leg tapers to 47mm at the top
D	2	Back legs*	Ash	76	76	1118	Each leg tapers to 47mm at the top
E	2	Side aprons	Ash	25	127–178	451	See illustration for details
F	1	Back apron	Ash	25	178	819	
G	2	Front rails	Ash	25	102	844	See illustration for details
H	1	Center divider	Ash	25	67	489	
J	1	Mounting plate	Plywood	19	76	76	Attach to back end of center divider
K	2	End cleats	Ash	22	22	445	
L	2	Front and back rungs	Ash	25	102	819	
M	2	Side rungs	Ash	25	102	451	
N	2	Drawers	Ash	67	397	489	
N-1	2	Fronts	Ash	19	67	397	
N-2	2	Backs	Ash	13	67	384	
N-3	4	Sides	Ash	13	67	483	
N-4	2	Bottoms	Birch ply	6	384	476	
P	2	Drawer runners	Ash	25	25	394	
Q	1	Center drawer runner	Ash	25	76	394	
R	4	Pencil tray bottoms	Ash	6	38	590	
S	2	Pencil tray front	Ash	6	35	590	
T	2	Pencil tray center	Ash	6	41	590	
U	2	Drawer pulls	Padauk	19	25	32	Any contrasting wood will work; see illustration for details

*Note: The legs are tapered on the two outside sides only. The inside sides are left square for ease of assembly.

[1] First, machine the legs using the tapering jig on the table saw. Since the tops of the legs are angled to match the pitch of the work surface, move over to the miter saw and cut the leg tops to the appropriate angle as shown here.

[2] Plane off the outside corners of the legs at a taper to add a lighter look and feel to the desk. You can do this with either a jointer or with a hand plane. The taper width at the bottom of the leg can be adjusted to whatever looks and feels right to your personal taste.

[3] To draw the curve of the rungs, begin by marking the width at the center of the piece. Then simply connect the two corners with the center mark by bending a strip of wood and tracing the line as shown here.

[4] If you don't have a doweling jig, a homemade jig is easy to make. The front rails are doweled to the front legs because biscuits wouldn't work. In this photo, the jig is referenced to the edge of the end of the rail with a block attached to the jig.

[5] In this photo, the reference block is removed and the edge of the jig is set on a pencil mark drawn where the edge of the rail will go.

[6] Assemble the top frame using biscuits. Be sure to set them back far enough so they won't show through when the angle on the edge of the top is cut.

[7] Glue up the rails, aprons, legs and rungs. Then attach the center divider, side runners and bottom runners. Take your time and make sure these parts all line up and are parallel to each other so that the drawers fit well.

TIP

When sanding, it helps to have a task light set up to create sharp shadows on the work. All imperfections can be seen and sanded out.

Detail showing the left apron and rear leg joint. The ⅛" x ⅛" reveal at the bottom of the apron adds a nice shadow line.

[8] Assemble the drawers as detailed in the tech art and cutting list. Pay particular attention to the locking mortise-and-tenon joint used at the front of the drawers (shown here). This joint is made using the table saw. Again, take your time and cut test pieces to get the fit just right.

[9] Add the drawer pulls of your choice. Here, I used hand-carved pulls with the tool marks still showing to add texture and character.

[10] After cutting the stool legs to size as per the cutting list, glue and screw them to the stool top plate. Note that the notches are cut at the same angle as the tops and bottoms of the legs.

[11] Mark the rungs for the stool in the same way you did for the desk. Then cut to shape. Remember that the ends of the rungs are cut at the same angle as the leg ends.

[12] Cut the seat to size. To create the bevel, use a band saw with its table tilted at an angle. Then attach the seat to the top plate.

[13] Construct the writing panel using the same methods as for the previous project. Attach it to the assembly with cleats and screws. Then finish the desk with three coats of clear catalyzed lacquer. A coat of wax on the drawer sides and the runners will let the drawers slide in and out smoothly.

suppliers & Sources

House of Tools, Ltd.
woodworking tools and hardware
100 Mayfield Common
Edmonton, Alberta, Canada T5P 4B3
800-661-3987
www.houseoftools.com

JessEm Tool Co.
Rout-R-Slide and Rout-R-Lift
171 Robert Street E #7 & #8
Penetanguishene, Ontario, Canada L9M 1G9
800-436-6799
www.jessem.com

Delta Machinery
woodworking machinery and accessories
4825 Highway 45 North
Jackson, TN 38305
800-438-2486
www.deltawoodworking.com

Porter-Cable
woodworking tools
4825 Highway 45 North
Jackson, TN 38302
800-487-8665
www.porter-cable.com

Richelieu Hardware
professional trade hardware supplies
7900 West Henri-Bourassa
Ville St-Laurent, Quebec, Canada H4S 1V4
800-361-6000
www.richelieu.com

Tenryu America, Inc.
saw blades
4301 Woodland Park Drive, Suite 104
West Melbourne, FL 32904
800-951-7297
www.tenryu.com

Rockler Woodworking and Hardware
woodworking tools and hardware
4365 Willow Drive
Medina, MN 55340
800-279-4441
www.rockler.com

Lee Valley Tools
woodworking tools and hardware
P.O. Box 1780
Ogdensburg, NY 13669-6780
800-267-8735
www.leevalley.com

Wolfcraft, Inc.
woodworking hardware
1222 W. Ardmore Avenue, P.O. Box 687
Itasca, IL 60143
630-773-4777
www.wolfcraft.com

Woodcraft Supply Corp.
woodworking hardware
1177 Rosemar Road
Parkersburg, WV 26101
800-225-1153
www.woodcraft.com

Woodworker's Hardware
woodworking hardware
P.O. Box 180
Sauk Rapids, MN 56379
800-383-0130

Adams & Kennedy
wood supply
6178 Mitch Owen Road, P.O. Box 700
Manotick, Ontario, Canada K4M 1A6
613-822-6800
www.adams-kennedy.com

Doug Mockett & Company, Inc.
computer furniture accessory hardware
P.O. Box 3333
Manhattan Beach, CA 90266
800-523-1269
www.mockett.com

[i n d e x]